TALES of a TRAMP

From Berlin to Sydney

JPF Manfred Richter

© Manfred Richter 2021

All rights reserved. Except for the quotation of short passages for the purposes of criticism and review, no part of this publication may be reproduced, stored in a retrieval system, or transmitted in any form or by any means, electronic, mechanical, photocopying, recording, or otherwise, without the prior written permission of the Copyright Authority Ltd. or the publisher.

First published in Australia October 2021
Layout and design by Clark & Mackay.

Printed by Clark and Mackay, Brisbane, Australia

Disclaimer

These are the personal travels of the author, and no disrespect is intended to other cultures.

I travel because I want to meet the people and experience the cultures of other countries.

Acknowledgement:

I would like to thank Angie Hoffmann for suggesting to write this book and for her help when I did.

Contents

About the Author vii

Chapter 1: Off to Cape Town, South Africa 1
    The first verse of the Koran 5
    Across the Desert 6
    Cairo Youth Hostel 13

Chapter 2: Climbing the Cheops (Khufu) Pyramid 15
    Cairo 15
    Sudan, Eritrea, and Ethiopia 41
    Axum 43

Chapter 3: Further Travels across East Africa 47
    Ethiopia 47

Chapter 4: Kenya 75
    Nairobi 75
    Moshi 80
    Kilimanjaro 82

Chapter 5: Tanzania 97
    Moshi 97
    Dar es Salaam 99

Chapter 6: South Africa 115
    Johannesburg 115

Chapter 7: Leaving South Africa 127
    Madagascar, Mon Amour 127
    Tananarive 130
    Ampefy 137

    Antsirabe 140

Chapter 8: Continuing Travels Around Madagascar 145
    Miandrivazo 145
    Marondave 149
    Across the Indian Ocean 154

Chapter 9: India 161
    Bombay (Mumbai) 162
    Express Train to Madras 166

Chapter 10: Ceylon 173
    Colombo 173
    The Rock of Sigiria 183
    Trincomalee 187
    Ferry to India 188
    Madras 189

Chapter 11: The Road to Kathmandu 205
    Kathmandu 208

Chapter 12: Travelling to Australia 229
    Bound for Botany Bay 229

About the Author

Peter and Manfred (author), 1964 in Berlin

My name is Manfred Richter, and I was an only child, born in Berlin, Germany, during the 2nd World War. After school, I undertook an apprenticeship as an accountant and studied accounting and Business English in night schools. Life with the Berlin Wall and political upheavals during the Cold War made me long for greener pastures. Holidays in Denmark and England, during that time, increased that longing.

In 1964, my friend, Peter Dumlich, suggested that we travel to Cape Town, South Africa, and start a new life there. I immediately agreed. Our friend, Axel Neisch, had an old Volkswagen that we thought we could use to commence our travels. We paid for a new motor and, for some time, saved as much money as possible. Finally, at the beginning of October in 1964, we took off. However, Peter went broke in Tunisia and returned to Berlin. He now lives on a farm in outback Canada. Axel explored Egypt and worked on a Kibbutz in Israel to save money for the trip home. Once he returned to Germany, he ran a shop in Berlin; passed away in June 2019.

From Tunisia, I decided to carry on by myself. I tramped to Cairo, worked with a German company in Egypt for two and a half years, and in 1967, flew to Ethiopia. In Addis Ababa, I met Max Gallmann, another 'tramp' from Switzerland. We got on well together, and from Christmas 1967, we hitch-hiked to South Africa. After a couple of years, we kept going and ended up in Australia in November 1970. In January 1972, I found my wife, Tisna, in Tonga. She already had five children of her own. Despite all odds, we got married and lived happily in Brisbane until she passed away in 2012.

CHAPTER 1:

Off to Cape Town, South Africa

It is the 4th of October 1964 in West Berlin, Germany. Peter, Axel, and I have put our rucksacks, photo bags, a few boxes, and a lot of spare parts into the old Volkswagen that belongs to Axel. The three of us had gone to the same class in school, and we were about the same age. It was the time of the hippies. We all had short hair, although mine was thinning already. None of us used drugs. Peter was strongly built and had travelled to Nepal on a motor scooter. He became our leader. I sat on the back seat of the car, had the maps on my knees, and guided us all the way to Tunisia.

Our parents were Germans. My parents were very worried when I told them about my travel plans, but they did not try to stop me. Some other relatives and acquaintances warned us we would get killed and be eaten by lions or bitten by snakes. Maybe some of them were jealous.

The manager of the company I worked for told me: "Why don't you prove yourself in Germany first?" To me, that would have been a waste of time.

Then, it is time to say goodbye to our parents; I still remember my mother crying and my father's worried face. We embrace our tearful

Axel on the left, Peter in the middle

Manfred in France

girlfriends for the last time and jump into the car. Axel energetically turns the engine on and puts his foot on the accelerator. As we pass the "Funkturm", Berlin's Eiffel Tower, we wonder when and if we will return on the other side of the road. We have endured life too long being surrounded by the Wall in Berlin and have longed for wider horizons. Hence, we three misfits are now making an escape from the "Island in the "Red Sea."

Under a cool and overcast sky, we leave the polluted air of the city behind us and race along the highway to the East German border. An officious police officer with his hated East German uniform has a look at our passports. He is not permitted to put a stamp in them. This is not an internationally recognised border. We have to unpack the car, open our bags, and answer all sorts of questions about our trip. When we have to show our money, Peter pulls a money bag from under his singlet. I open my zipper. The bag is in my pants. A police lady seems to be embarrassed and leaves the room. This procedure lasts for one and a half hours. It makes us even happier to leave a divided Germany.

Soon our little beetle, with three boyhood friends in it, cruises full speed along the Autobahn towards the Black Forest in the Southwest of Germany. We pass Brunswick, Hannover, Hamm, and other cities. Finally, as twilight is descending, we stop off to stay with friends in a village for the night.

The next morning, it's an early start, and the cool air makes us wish we had warming air conditioning in our little beetle. After Frankfurt, Heidelberg, and Karlsruhe, we enter the Black Forest and its mountain ranges; we spend the night in our tent on a camp site.

Another day takes us through the mountain scenery of Switzerland. At the French border, we have to ask an uninterested customs officer to put a date stamp into our passports as a souvenir.

Along the Rhone valley, the road gets narrow and climbs into mountains. As we head into the alpine town of Lyon, France, traffic is dense. Peter and Axel have to concentrate on the steering wheel to avoid an accident. We have another rainy and cold night in our tent on a farm along the River Rhone. We pass Avignon, and four days after our departure from Berlin, we reach the southern port city of Marseille.

We don't stop there, though, and follow the road along the coast that takes us to Barcelona, Spain. We turn right after that and on 25 October, we reach the capital city, Madrid. On the way, we fill our flasks with local red wine and munch the long French baguettes with olives and goat cheese. Three happy travellers enjoy breathing the warm air of the South.

The next stopover is Toledo, in central Spain, before we enter Portugal at Badajoz. Lisbon, the capital of Portugal, keeps us entertained for a few days. It is a beautiful old city with many cheap restaurants and yummy food. Then, on the 4th of November, we put our Volkswagen on a ferry from Gibraltar to Ceuta in Morocco, North Africa. It is exactly one month and after just over 5,000 kilometres that we reach the shores of Africa. The first section of our long trip to South Africa has been completed. We are looking forward to exploring some countries on another continent.

After some adventures in Morocco and the neighbouring country of Algeria, we arrive in Tunisia, situated east of Algeria, and the capital of Tunis, at the southern end of the Mediterranean Sea's Gulf of Tunis. In a cheap guest house, Peter counts his money and finds out that he is broke. Axel is not much better off. They decide to take the car by ferry to Taormina, on the island of Sicily, where Peter's mother lives. He visits her and returns to Berlin to marry a girl from Tasmania, Australia and then, moves to Canada. In 2019, he is still living on a farm far away from city life and political problems.

I feel a bit lonely after my friends have left and suppress a few tears of anger. Later on, Axel will obtain some more funds from home and meets me again in Cairo, but, for the moment, I have to make my own way. So, I get rid of half the contents of my rucksack, spend some time reading my little Bible—a souvenir from my girlfriend—and make my way to the main road. The thumb of my right hand points to the South whenever a car appears. This is the day on which I become an adult: from now on, I don't follow others, because as the captain of my own ship, I am now able to steer it into the direction of my own choice. I also have to accept the results of my own decisions.

After some time, a car stops and offers me a lift. It drops me after forty kilometres. I start walking along the main road of a small village and come across an empty chair on the footpath. I sit down next to my rucksack. Friendly and smiling people bring me a cup of tea which is very welcome. Soon, a truck stops. The driver, after hearing that I want to continue travelling further south, offers to take me. He puts my bag on top of the cabin, pulls my bush knife from my rucksack, and places it at my feet. I am embarrassed at this kind gesture. It is the start of a 400kilometre journey to the Oasis of Gabes, in the South of Tunisia. By the time I arrive there, I have forgotten our little Volkswagen and the feeling of betrayal by my two friends who left me so unexpectedly. However, I still dream of Cape Town.

The first verse of the Koran

Walking around Gabes, in Tunisia, makes me hungry. In a small restaurant, I eat chicken on spaghetti. After suffering from my first dysentery in Africa, I have to eat something different from couscous and African noodle soups.

It is a quintessential North African scene, as from the Minaret of a Mosque, the Muezzin calls people to come for evening prayers: "Allah u Akbar!" The echoing voice from the loudspeaker can be heard far away. I join the crowd and make my way to the Mosque.

I use my few words of French and ask an old man: *"Salaam, Monsieur. Entrée pour moi possible?"*

He shakes his head.

Next, I try a young man who looks well educated. He asks me to follow him. I take off my mountain boots, put them next to the sandals of the locals, and squat on the mats which cover the floor. The Muezzin praises Allah and reads the first verse of the Koran. My neighbours are surprised when they hear me reciting the original text. I have picked it up from a German tramp who once learned it in West Pakistan.

The movements that require the up and down of hands and body while praying is easy for me. First, one holds the hands behind the ears, listens to the voice of Allah, and then holds them in front of the face, as if reading the Koran. Then, one bends forward and holds the hands on the knees, squats on the heels, and finally kneels down and touches the floor with the forehead.

Lots of smelly feet have stood on the mats before me. I wrinkle my nose but, it gives me a chance to enjoy the odour of the 'Big Wide World' and the holes in the socks of the believer in front of me. Many prayers that follow are accompanied by harmonious singing. I regret that I did not bring my tape recorder.

When the service is finished, people sit around me and ask me to repeat the prayer again and again: *"Bis millahhirr. Rach maneerRahim…"*

They ask if I am a German Muslim.

"Sorry, I am not," I reply. But I tell them that I respect other faiths and that I agree there can only be one god. There are just many names for him and different ways to approach him. Grateful smiles are the reaction.

It's time for me to continue on my travels. Hitch-hiking to Libya is no problem. At the border, I sleep on my air mattress under the customs office counter. A friendly police officer borrows my torchlight and uses it to help him look for smugglers in the desert at night.

Across the Desert
Libya, 01.12.64

After a few days in Tripoli, the capital of Libya, it is time to continue my travel to Egypt. I only have a few traveller's cheques left, which is concerning. Amer Izzawi, a travel agent in Tripoli, seems to like me and pays for a seat in a little Opel bus which takes me over a distance of 1,200 kilometres to Benghazi, a seaside town in eastern Libya. I find a garage where I can sleep on the floor.

During the 2nd World War, Benghazi (Italian – Bengasi) was completely destroyed. Therefore, most of the houses are newly built. Little is left of the old town. After a short walk around, I lift the rucksack on the shoulders and head for the main road. By midday, a Landrover stops, and the driver offers me a ride to Derna, a distance of 300 kilometres.

Karl from Canada

On the way, the driver picks up another 'tramp'. His name is Karl, a Canadian Art Student who wants to study the ancient monuments of Egypt.

Soon after Bengazhi, the desert landscape changes. The road crosses a plateau with trees and fields with agricultural crops and cows. Just before we reach the small town of Derna, the road winds down to the coast again.

Karl and I decide to keep hiking together. We reach Derna in the evening. But, as there is no more traffic—hence no more hitchhiking—we cannot carry on to Tobruk, the original destination. As there does not seem to be any hostel, we go to a police station where they let us sleep on the floor and provide us with drinking water.

The next morning, we thank the police for the free accommodation. Heading outside, we are hopeful of catching a lift and start walking up the road, a truck, and afterwards, a mobile crane of the Royal Air

Force of Great Britain takes us along for twenty kilometres. After waiting a while, finally, a car stops and carries us all the way to Tobruk on the coast in eastern Libya.

Like in Benghazi, the houses in Tobruk are new. The war must have left a landscape of ruins here. The town lies on the slope of a hill with a view over a beautiful natural harbour. On the far side of the bay is the German war cemetery. It looks like a fortress with its high walls, which are 80 m long. On all four corners are round towers. In the middle of the court, the fallen soldiers have been buried under marble slabs and, around the walls, the names of the soldiers are listed. Nearby are the cemeteries of British and French soldiers. All around is a desert landscape with gravel, a few bushes, and bare hills. What a forsaken place to fight and die in the stinking desert heat with flies in eyes and ears and fleas jumping all over the place … What human madness raged here where nature is the actual enemy! It seems as if the whole landscape is frozen stiff in death.

The traffic, too, seems to have died, and we wait around patiently, waving our hands in front of our faces against the flies. It is late in the afternoon before a Red Cross van arrives and offers to take us along to the Libyan border with Egypt. From there, we find a car that gives us a lift across the fifteen kilometres wide no-man's land to the border post of Egypt. However, the customs officers have gone home, and it is too late for us to be processed. Searching the nearby buildings, we find a bathroom in a school and sleep on the floor. The howling of a sandstorm around us provides the unusual music for the night.

In the morning, a truck carries us fifty kilometres towards Marsamatru, into the Western Desert of Egypt. Dropping us off, it leaves the road and disappears behind some sand hills. We sit by the road with our rucksacks, left alone in the middle of nowhere.

Soon, the sky gets dark. It looks like an early night. A storm starts. The sand of the desert is moving. Clouds of dust and sand envelop us. There is no place where we can hide. I pull the hat over

Egypt 1964

my forehead and cover my nose and mouth with a handkerchief. But I still breathe sand, bite on the sand, and spit sand. One can see only for a few metres. Then, my eyes are full of sand too, and I am unable to see anything at all. We kneel next to our rucksacks—trying to find some shelter from the howling dust storm—pulling our heads between our shoulders.

Then, the thunder and lightning arrives. Rain starts falling. The sand gets wet and changes into wet putty. I want to take photos and swear because the films in both cameras are finished. I finally find a plastic bag for the camera and put a new film in it with one hand while I hold the bag closed with the other. That's how I keep the camera dry while I get wet. I hope the photos will turn out all right.

We are lucky that the rain does not turn into a cloud burst. But our clothes are soaking wet. Then, the sky calms down. Some light appears on the horizon. Clouds and sky appear in all varieties of blue. The wind pushes the clouds over the nearby sea. The rumbling in the clouds continues while a sinking sun bursts through and paints a rainbow over the desert.

Rainbow after the storm

Our Bedouin hosts

The Army truck

Suddenly life returns to the landscape. The thorn bushes appear to be greener. The ground takes on a rich golden yellow hue. Birds lift themselves up with beating wings into the evening sky, singing, and then, they disappear into the distance.

Two Bedouins riding on their donkeys appear on the road. They seem to feel sorry for us as they stop and get off their animals. They collect some twigs, start a fire, and cook tea for the "BedouiniAlemani" (German Bedouins). They feed us with Egyptian flat bread and peanuts. Such is the hospitality of the desert! Afterwards, they offer to let us ride on their donkeys. Tramping on donkeys would be a new experience but, Karl and I prefer to wait for cars to take us out of the desert.

Then, darkness descends. We have to think about making our bed in the wet desert sand. Suddenly, like a Fata Morgana—a mirage of a non-existing item caused by reflections in the sky just above the horizon—the truck which gave us a lift earlier appears again.

Like an old camel with a heavy load, it stumbles towards us, along the track, and crawls up onto the road. The truck is loaded with bags full of sand and stones, maybe to fortify the border with Israel. It stops, but we see that there is no room in the cabin. We lift the rucksacks on our shoulders, and jumping up and over the bonnet, we climb onto the load. We fasten ourselves plus the rucksacks as firmly as possible to the ropes which hold the load together.

The driver hands us two blankets to protect us from the chilly night air. Then the 'diesel' camel slowly rumbles on into the night. Due to the heavy load, the truck can only travel at a speed of twenty kilometres. It will take us a while to travel the 150 kilometres to Marsamatru, and this means we will have to endure eight hours on the sandbags.

Nevertheless, we feel quite comfortable lying on the uneven bags. Everything is moving … the truck, our thoughts, the road on which we roll, and the indefinite expanse of the star-covered sky. Life appears strange and small in the quiet of the night in a lifeless desert, under the majestic height of the black sky with stars that look like shiny diamonds. Karl opens a bottle of brandy. We drink it very slowly, as we are gently jostled by the moving vehicle, and while we sing Boy Scout songs in English and German.

It is imperative not to lift the heads. Every now and then, telegraph wires hang across the road which could pull us down from our heightened position that would result in a hard landing on the tar of the road. The night seems to be endless but, our truck keeps rolling onwards. Twice, there is a tea break in tin shacks by the side of the road. We eat Egyptian flat bread with fish and beans from cans. Our driver, with some excitement, draws a swastika in the sand with his finger and tells us stories about General Rommel, the German general of WWII while we get roasted by the sun on the tin roof of the tin shack. Germans seem to be popular here. The Arabs seem to ignore that Karl is Canadian although with a German name. I belong to a new generation and try to forget the horrors of the past.

Finally, we arrive in Marsamatru and again spend the rest of the night on the floor of a police station. The next day, Karl and I sit patiently on the side of the road until the afternoon when a jeep stops and takes us along to Alexandria; a distance of 260 kilometres. On arrival, a crowd of curious people gathers around us. They ask for our nationality. When I say *"Aleman"* (German) they clap their hands. A tea vendor lifts his arm and says, *"Heil Hitler."* Then, from the tank on his back, he pours a couple of cups of sweet tea and hands them to us as a welcome present.

Cairo Youth Hostel

We shoulder our rucksacks and, with some effort, find our way to the local Youth Hostel.

A couple of empty bunks are free for us. After the discomfort on the concrete floor in the police stations, we enjoy having a long sleep on soft mattresses. It has taken me three months to travel from Berlin to Cairo.

The next morning, we take a train to Cairo, where I am surprised to meet Axel again, who had the address of the Youth Hostel. A few days later, against all odds, and with a bribe for an immigration officer, I find a job with a German civil engineering company for which I have worked in Berlin. Work only has to start at the beginning of the New Year so, I have time to explore Cairo.

Manfred and Axel in Cairo, Midan al Tahrir, Dec. 1964

CHAPTER 2:

Climbing the Cheops (Khufu) Pyramid

Cairo
3.12.1964

I have three goals in Africa. I want to climb the Cheops Pyramid (Egypt), stand on top of Mount Kilimanjaro on the border between Tanzania and Kenya, and spit into the sea at the Cape of Good Hope (South Africa). Today, I plan to reach my first goal. It is only a short bus trip from Midan al Tahrir in the city that separates me from it. Bus number eight to Giza arrives but does not stop completely. No one waits for people to get out. Climbing into a bus during morning rush hour in Cairo is a battle for survival. I have watched a rugby game final on TV and remember how the players formed a scrum. So, I decide to be the ball.

I do not manage to get up onto the first bus. But when the next one arrives, I jump between the opposing parties, hold on to my camera bag with my left arm, and protect my face with my right arm.

The people behind me push me into the crowd who want to get off the bus. My mountain boots step on feet wearing only plastic

Pancake bar at Midan al Tahrir

sandals. Somehow, I end up on the platform in the back of the bus under which the motor sits. I pull up my legs and feel safe. Outside the window behind me are the faces of fellows who hang on the back of the bus; they are flat like bed bugs with their fingers on the window frame and their feet on the bumper bar. It feels like travelling in a can of sardines.

The trip to Giza takes half an hour. In the meantime, I smell garlic around me, and I hurriedly pull up my collar when someone next to me coughs and spits. I watch a mother in the open door holding on to the door frame with one hand whilst she holds her suckling baby with the other. All the time, the bus races onwards through clouds of dust. In disbelief, I watch as a pervert in his nightgown-like Jelabia rubs his prick against the shoulder of a little girl until his gaze disappears into Nirvana. No one notices it with the passengers squeezed together like sardines, all holding onto the rails under the roof of the swerving bus. When he gets off the bus, the girl has tears in her eyes.

But maybe, I am the only one who saw it. At one stage, the arm of the conductor appears above the heads. I show him an Egyptian pound note which he cannot change. He lets me travel for free.

When the bus arrives at the end station, I jump out and end up in a crowd of tour guides, camel riders, money changers, and souvenir vendors. I get rid of them by using my recently learned Egyptian swear word, *"Mafish flus. Ana meskin. Yalla imschi."* This means, "I have no money. I am poor. Quick, piss off."

The Cheops (Khufu) Pyramid is nearby. I stand in front of it. I thought it would be higher. With its height of 136 m, it equals the height of the *"Funkturm"* (RadioTower in Berlin). The massive pile of carefully sorted rocks is certainly impressive. In order to show my respect for the Pharaohs, I decide to climb the pyramid. That is not easy. I have been told that the last tourist who fell down was an Australian.

From a safe distance, I study the rocks with my binoculars. They are covered with the sand of thousands of years of desert storms. At one of the northern corners of the Cheops Pyramid, the sand has been wiped off to make the climb possible for tourists. A signboard clearly indicates that "Climbing is forbidden without a guide". There is also a charge of 25 Piasters; that is too expensive for me. I will make my way up by myself so that I can stay up there as long as I like. I don't know if one gets arrested for climbing alone but, I would not mind a night in jail for this adventure.

At the bottom of the pyramid, the rocks are often shoulder-high. Further up, they appear to get smaller … about knee-high. The space on each rock is no more than 50 cm, not much to stop a fall. And there is no handrail. It takes some patience to wait until the police nearby go into their office and the tour guides argue with some tourists. By the time they notice me and call for the cops, I am already twenty metres up, and cheekily, I can afford to wave at them and give them a friendly smile.

Photo Above: Coffee bar for poor tramps
Photo Top Right: Tourist "Staircase"
Photo Right: Warning sign.
Photo Below: Cheops Pyramid platform

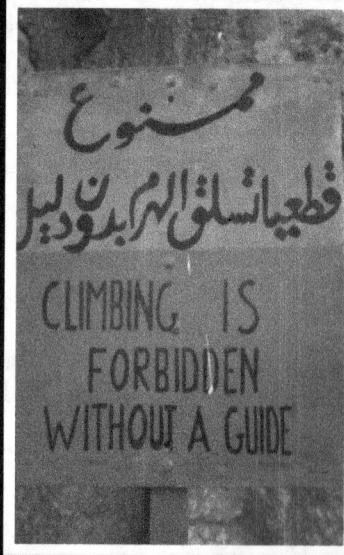

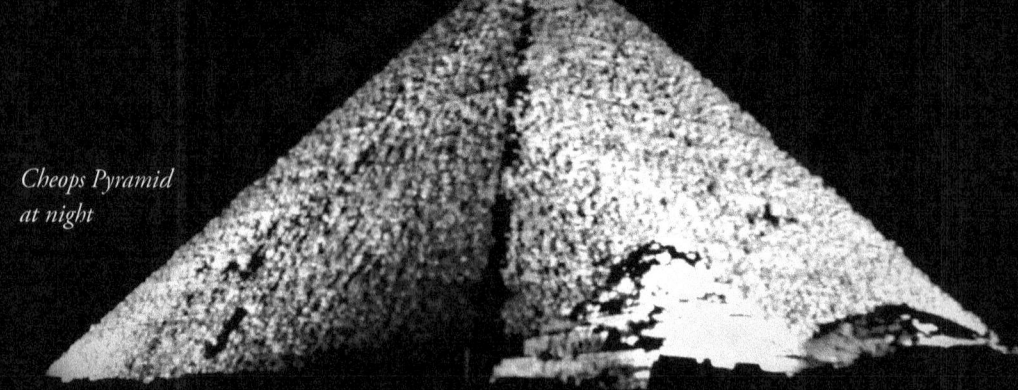

Cheops Pyramid at night

Climbing the Cheops (Khufu) Pyramid

I really enjoy climbing on my knees while my hands hold onto the next block. Every now and then, I sit down and look around to become adjusted to the height and take in the view. Sometimes, the rocks are partly broken, or they are covered with sand. But I climb up on the "tourist corner" where the stones have been cleaned. It takes me twenty minutes to cover the 200m to the top; not bad for a beginner. I have been told that Egyptian guides can do it in six minutes.

The platform of the pyramid is completely covered with the names of previous climbers who have chiselled their names into the stones over hundreds of years. No one has ever found out if the rocks on top formed a point like on other pyramids. A pole marks the theoretical height.

Standing there fills me with awe and makes me sit down. I imagine that the thousands of years on which I stand are metres and, suddenly, I feel much closer to God. *Am I not on the largest altar mankind has ever built for God?* Maybe one day, a man will land on the Moon and thereby continue the dreams of the Pharaohs! From the west, the evening sun shines across the Libyan Desert. It appears to be a seemingly endless sea of sand and rocks, and it drowns the Mukattam Mountains and Cairo, in the east, in a hue of golden light.

In between, from north to south, is a wide area of green rice fields framing the Nile on its never-ending flow to the Mediterranean Sea.

The Pharaohs built the pyramids at the edge of the desert like a symbol of the struggle against death. They had their bodies mummified and took all their worldly goods with them into the grave. The mummies of the Pharaohs are still popular in this world even after thousands of years. But, in the heaven of the ancient Egyptians, I imagine that their traces have become lost.

While I am daydreaming on the top of the Cheops Pyramid, a storm pushes black clouds across the Delta and rips the rain from them. I have heard that this happens only four or five times a year.

Looking down from the Cheops Pyramid

Mastabas (graves) for senior Pharaohs

So, I squat behind a rock and enjoy the drenching. However, the rain makes the rocks and the sand on them slippery. Soon, it will be dark. It is time to return to earth and human life. As I look down, I suddenly have a sick feeling in my stomach, and for a minute, I have to fight a panic attack. But then, I take my boots and socks off, hang them around my neck, and start gliding carefully from rock to rock on my wet 'behind', making sure my feet rest safely on the next stone.

As I descend, the wind is blowing and helps to dry the surfaces of the rocks. Closer to the bottom of the pyramid, I start jumping from rock to rock and am cheered on by a crowd of school children. As I jump onto the ground, they surround me as if I am a film star. Their teacher hits them with his fists to make room for me.

A dragoman on his camel blocks my way and wants to sell me a ride to the bus stop. When I refuse, he pulls at my hair, and I quickly grab his foot and try to twist him from the saddle. The camel jumps aside and saves the situation. Nearby sits my Canadian mate, Karl. He is smoking his pipe and welcomes me back with a big grin on his face. It is then that I remember that I had hoped to write my Christmas cards on top of the pyramid … But, as I have forgotten to take a ballpoint pen, I would not have been able to do this, anyhow. We decide to return to Giza tomorrow.

Giza
16.12.1964

Karl and I take an early bus to Giza. Before climbing the Great Pyramid of Giza we explore the inside. That costs us five Piasters. We pretend to belong to a group of American tourists. It saves us the *baksheesh* (payment) for the guided tour. But the guide is suspicious because we don't want to have our photo taken sitting on a camel with Egyptian head gear. He turns away when we exclaim repeatedly, "OK" and "Isn't it nice!"

The entrance is in the middle of the pyramid, not far from the ground. This time, there is a handrail as we enter the gate into the underworld. The tunnel is narrow and low. There is little air for breathing, and a neon light fills the claustrophobic space. We start sweating immediately.

I have to return to the German text for a while, as it is hard to translate the rhymes:

"Vor mir in dem Blondgesicht zerfliessen Rouge und Puderschicht. Es geht bergab und dann bergauf – zur Königinkammer im Entenlauf. Der Führer spricht. Die Menge lauscht und ist vom Schweißgeruch berauscht. Sodann auf einer Hühnerleiter geht es zur Königskammer weiter. Man schiebt sich hoch, man schnauft und stöhnt. Man ist des Kletterns ganz entwöhnt. Jetzt wird as eng. Jetzt wird es flach. Die Menge drückt von hinten nach. Und wo zwei Steine stehn hervor, stößt mancher sich noch Kopf und Ohr. Und so mit manchem "Weh" und "Ach" folgt man dem Fremdenführer nach. Der Raum ist weit. Der Raum ist groß. "Mein Gott, wo sitzt der Büstenhalter bloß?" Aus schwarzem Stein sind Wand und roof. "Ach wäre man doch waterproof!" Man schwitzt und lehnt sich an den Sarkophag. Ob hier der Pharao einst lag? Da zucken Blitze kreuz und quer von einem Fotografenheer. "Look honey, auch der Großpapa stand mal an jener Stelle da!" – "Attention" ruft der Dragoman und strengt dann seine Stimme an. Die Stimme schallt. Das Echo rollt. "How nice!" sagt man ganz ungewollt. Und dann marschiert man heiter hinab again die Hühnerleiter. Ach wäre man doch endlich raus aus diesem heissen Affenhaus! Doch was kommt dort? Man kann es raten. Ein ganzer Trupp UN-Soldaten. Man stellt sich quer. Man macht sich dünn. Zum Ausgang kommt nun keiner hin. Das schiebt und schwitzt und drängt und lacht. Vor manchem Auge wird es Nacht. Ich weiß nicht wie es weiter ging und wie

wir raus gekommen. Doch draußen hat der Dragoman von uns kein Geld bekommen."

After a rest, it is time to climb the outside of the pyramid. Karl does not trust his climbing skills and does not follow me. However, he pretends that he wants to climb and saves me from a whole lot of tour guides who rush at him. When they finally notice me climbing, they leave me alone. Maybe they think, "Let that idiot kill himself!" But, I take my time and avoid any risk. When I reach the top, I sit down to enjoy the view. The morning sun is beautiful and warm. I write my postcards and play some German tunes on my mouth organ to honour the Pharaohs. Then, I place my camera bag under my head and enjoy a nap. Afterwards, I study the surroundings with my binoculars. Nearby is the Chefren (Kafre) Pyramid. It has about the same height as Cheops but appears to be a bit higher because it sits on an elevated plateau. Unfortunately, I will not be able to play my mouth organ over there because it is forbidden to climb that pyramid.

The top of the Chefren Pyramid still has the original sandstone cover and so, it is too dangerous to climb. The last of this group of pyramids is the step Pyramid of Mykerinos, maybe the oldest of them. It is only 62 m high and cannot be climbed.

All over the place are graves, temples of the dead, and small pyramids for the relatives and government officials of the Pharaohs. The mummies rested peacefully at the bottom of deep shafts until they were disturbed by grave robbers, archaeologists, and tourists.

Far in the distance, one can recognise the step Pyramids of Sakkara. The oldest of them was built about 2,600 BC, and as per Wikipedia and other sources, it is known as "the first large stone construction in the world". And then, it is time to have a look at the Sphinx.

Chefren (Khafre) Pyramid with original sandstone cover

Giza, 16.12.1964

After climbing the pyramid, Karl and I explore the surroundings until it gets dark. We make our way to the Sphinx to watch the "Greatest Show of the World." In front of the Sphinx, is a platform with chairs where tourists—for an expensive entrance fee—can watch the spectacle. The Egyptians call it *"Son et Lumiere"* and President Nasser, on 13.4.1961, made a speech during the opening ceremony.

Karl and I climb a rocky ledge where we lie flat on our bellies and watch the show for free.

In order to get close to the Sphinx to take the photo, I had to get through a fence. I showed my German Youth Hostel card to the guard, said "German Press International", gave him a little tip, and he opened the door.

I have to return to the German text for a while, as it is hard to translate the rhymes:

> *Abends nach des Tages Würme ziehen die Touristenschwürme an der Wüste Rand. Dort dann lauschen sie auf Stühlen jenen Ton- und Zauberspielen, die als „Ton und Licht" bekannt. „Was*

Climbing the Cheops (Khufu) Pyramid

View from the tourist platform

wird kommen?" hört man's munkeln – während schon die Sterne funkeln über'm Pharaonental. Jeder blickt nur auf das Eine, auf die Pyramidensteine, und das Warten wird zur Qual. „Was wird uns die Sphinx wohlsagen? Was sind König Cheops' Klagen? Was hat Chefren einst erlebt?" Und man lehnt sich an die Stühle. Mancher zittert in der Kühle, während sich ein Wind erhebt.

Doch nun öffnet sich die Szene! Metro-Goldwyn-Mayer-Töne hallen kraftvoll durch die Nacht. Über viele Megaphone spricht dann eine Amazone von der Pharaonenpracht. Heute soll zu neuem Leben sich die alte Welt erheben. Technisch zeichnet „Philips France." Was bisher noch nie gelungen wird in Dur und Moll gesungen. Lauscht dem Pharaonentanz! Wührend so die Töne schwellen, in der Nähe Hunde bellen. Eine Lady will schon gehn.

Plötzlich füllt aus vielen Lampen grelles Licht auf jene Rampen, wo die Pyramiden stehn. Zahlreich sind die Leuchteffekte, die man für die Sphinx entdeckte. Ganz verlegen schaut sie drein. Und es staunt der Mond am Himmel über all das Farbgewimmel auf dem sonst so bleichen Stein.

Translated into English

In the evening, after the warmth of the day, the swarms of tourists move to the edge of the desert. There, they sit on chairs and listen to the sound and magic show known as "Sound and Light".

"What's coming?" You can hear them guessing, while the stars twinkle over the Pharaonic valley. Everyone only looks at one thing, the stones of the pyramids, and the waiting almost becomes torture.

"What will the Sphinx tell us? What are King Cheops grievances? What did Chefren once experience?" They lean against the chairs. Some shiver in the coolness while a wind appears.

But now the scene opens! Metro Goldwyn Mayer tones resound powerfully through the night. An Amazon then speaks of the

Pharaohs' splendour over many megaphones. Today, the old world will rise to new life. The technical design was made by Philips France. What has never been successfully sung in the past can now be heard in major and minor. Listen to the dance of the Pharaohs! While the sounds swell, dogs bark nearby. Amongst the crowd, a lady stands up; it looks like she wants to leave already.

Suddenly, many lamps pour bright lights onto the ramps of the pyramids. The light effects that have been set up for the Sphinx are plenty and she is suddenly in the spotlight. She looks very embarrassed. In my mind, I imagine that even the moon, as it looks down, is amazed at all the swarms of colourful lights reflected from the normally pale stones.

Sound and light for the Sphinx

Viel Papyr' und Hiroglyphen mussten weise Männer prüfen. Und nun spielt man es vom Band – wie die Pharaonen hausten, wie sie liebten, wie sie schmausten – hier in diesem Land. Wie sie kämpften, wie sie litten, wie sie schossen wenn sie ritten, wie sie starben ab und an.

Eine Stimme tönt voll Jammer aus Herrn Cheops Grabeskammer, und Herr Chefren schliesst sich an. Bald erschallen Geisterrufe an des Totentempels Stufe, und der Pharao erscheint. Hei, da jauchzt des Volkes Menge! Und man spürt, daß das Gedränge fast das Tonband bersten lässt. Welch ein Schreien, welch ein Jubel! Hufe klappern in dem Trubel. Welch ein Kitsch ist dieses Fest!

Doch es soll noch besser kommen. Denn die Sphinx, vom Lärm benommen, meldet sich zum Wort. Ringsum wird es Nacht und Schweigen, und die Sphinx die muss nun zeigen, wie der Schmerz noch in ihr bohrt. „Liebster!"stöhnen ihre Lippen, und ganz blau sind ihre Rippen, als von Caesar sie erzählt.

Translated into English

Wise men had to examine a lot of papyrus and hieroglyphs. And now, it is played from the tape: how the pharaohs lived; how they loved; how they feasted in this country; how they fought; how they suffered; how they shot when they rode; how they died now and then.

A voice full of misery comes from Mr Cheops' burial chamber, and Mr Chefren joins him. Soon the screams of ghosts can be heard from the steps of the temple of the dead, and the pharaoh appears.

The crowd begins to cheer! And, one can almost feel the noise that almost bursts the tape. What screaming, what jubilation! Hooves rattle in the hustle and bustle. This festival is really quite 'kitsch'!

But it gets even better ... For the Sphinx, dazed by the noise, speaks up. All around, it is night and we are surrounded by silence. The Sphinx must show how the pain is still ever-present, boring into her.

"Dearest!" Her lips moan, and her ribs are completely blue when she talks about Caesar.

Und der Caesar spielt die Lyre zur Musik von Goldwyn-Mayer bis er sich mit ihr vermählt. Ja, in jenen Zeiten hatte man noch Oberweiten! Seht Euch doch die Sphinx mal an! Auch die schöne Nefertit singt da noch ein Liedchen mit – seufzend dann und wann.

So vergeht fast eineStunde bis die Pharaonenkunde intensiv verbreitet ist. Dann verfinstert sich die Stätte, und ich halte jede Wette: Es war grosser Mist!

Translated into English

And Caesar plays the lyre to the music by Goldwyn-Mayer until he marries her. Yes, in those times they still had bust sizes! Take a look at the Sphinx … The beautiful Nefertiti also sings a little song—sighing every now and then.

Almost an hour passes before the stories of the Pharaoh's have been spread intensively. Then, the place darkens, and I will counter every bet … It was a lot of crap!

Cairo
17.12.1964
On the way back to the Youth Hostel in Cairo, a young Egyptian lawyer invites me in for tea at his home. I don't trust him, but I am intrigued and so, I agree. He introduces me to his father and his fiancée. Then, he asks me if I can organise an invitation and a work contract from a company in Germany. It does not matter what type of work it is. Anything goes, in order to get out of Egypt … Unfortunately, I can't help him. It is a typical question. One hears it often in Egypt.

Since the Revolution by Army Officers against King Farouk in 1952, better schooling has resulted in a new middle class developing.

This includes shop owners, bus drivers, police officers, and all who attend university. By the way, a second school education is sufficient to gain a university entrance.

During the university years, people learn not only reading and writing but thinking as well. That is where the conflict starts. They learn foreign languages and are now able to learn about the way of life in industrialised countries. They realise that beyond the borders, there is a different world by reading newspapers, going to the movies, or meeting tourists. They compare the 'outside' world with their own environment and realise how little material wealth and luxuries Egypt can offer them. It results in discontent, a loss of hope, and a complex of inferiority towards the foreigner. Then, this brings up the questions of how to escape from the sad environment? How to get to Germany, Canada, Australia, or the USA, so as to assimilate and start a new life? They are prepared to sacrifice their family and even forget about their religion for this goal.

The government does not encourage this loss of educated people. Egyptians are not supposed to talk to foreigners. Overseas travel is very hard to obtain due to a lack of foreign funds. People who manage to go overseas as students or on a work contract are considered lucky. But there is a punishment: those who migrate will not be permitted to return. They lose their country and family forever. Hence, the dream of the big wide world still remains a dream.

Egypt has also managed to get rid of their British and French supervisors and made friends with the Soviet Union. This means that an economy of scarcity has taken over. The shop windows are empty. Even basic food items like meat and bread are sometimes hard to come by. It feels like I have moved into East Germany or worse.

Ismailia
18.12.1964

I decide to visit friends in Ismailia, east of Cairo. I take my heavy rucksack along and travel in third class (Class 3) by train. It is hard to buy a ticket. The guy who sells the tickets stares at me in disbelief. Most Europeans travel first or second class. Well, I am the exception. Travelling this way gives me a chance to mix with ordinary people; they are the majority after all.

Travelling to Ismailia is not very different from Cairo. Few people travel on the steps outside the train doors. The luggage rails run along the walls above the windows. One has to be determined to find and fit into a space up there between bags, baskets, and bundles of clothes. It means being able to sleep in a "bed" in third class. Up there, I am relatively safe from pickpockets and from people spitting on my feet. Someone wrote on the wall in Arabic "Hotel for sleeping".

Usually, one has to climb into the train through the windows because, at the doors, there are battles going on between people who want to get out and the ones who want to get in. I manage to step into the train with my heavy rucksack only because one carriage is reserved for school children. The teachers seem to be interested in me and let me enter through the door. A screaming and laughing crowd of school kids shouting questions descend upon me. The teachers 'help' me by smacking the kids, punching them with fists, and kicking them with their shoes. I even get my torch back from one little thief who managed to knock it off from the rucksack.

At one of the next stations, some soldiers and farmers manage to climb onboard. The teachers roll up their sleeves. A battle ensues with fists and sticks accompanied by a lot of yelling and screaming because the car is reserved for the school children. The farmers end up back on the platform, and the soldiers settle down on the luggage rails. I hang my legs over my rucksack and squeeze into a corner. The next incident begins with the voice of a blind woman rising above all the other noise. She is trying to sell combs until she stumbles and falls over luggage in the corridor. The ticket collector is accompanied by a guard … maybe to make sure he does not get bribed or robbed. A tea vendor is like an acrobat, as he successfully balances full tea glasses through the wildly shaking carriage.

I arrive in Ismailia late in the afternoon and make my way to the guesthouse of my future employer (Hochtief AG). As I exit onto the balcony from my room, I take in the beautiful view over the city and the Suez Canal.

19.12.1964

Back in Cairo, I stroll around the streets until it is night. When the neon lights shine, and the shop windows are illuminated, Cairo changes its face. Poverty and misery seem to disappear into the back streets. The sidewalks are crowded with people in suits and neckties; some ladies wear high heels, and some blouses permit a glimpse into their content. It is the time of long queues outside cinemas, of crowded tea shops and restaurants.

In this Moslem country, some shops even have Christmas decorations and a cardboard Father Christmas holding a card saying, "Merry Christmas" and *"Bonne Année"*.

At street corners, one can buy plants that look a bit like Christmas trees. The Lufthansa Airline window even has a properly decorated German Christmas tree. For the first time, I feel a little bit homesick. There even is a small German Lutheran Church where I plan to attend a service at Christmas.

I also notice that synagogues have a police guard for protection. The government policy is only focused on the State of Israel, not against the religion.

During my stay in Egypt, I will get arrested twice by the Military Secret Service. They suspect that I am a Jewish spy. It is dangerous to walk about and take photos. I tell them off.

Climbing the Cheops (Khufu) Pyramid

Taxi in Fayoum Oasis

But they say, "We trust the old Germans (Nazis) but not the young ones."

They let me go after I surrender the film from my camera. With some effort, I will get it back. The Israeli Intelligence Service will hardly be interested in belly dancing photos. I am lucky because I don't have to show my customs declaration. My two cameras are not on the list as they could get confiscated. I plan to sell them on the black market if I run out of money.

The Stock Exchange is closed permanently, a result of the Soviet-style economy favoured by President Nasser. At night, the Stock Exchange is the backdrop for black market traders who buy and sell US dollars for Egyptian pounds. For US dollars in cash or traveller's cheques, one can get twice as many Egyptian pounds as in the bank. Sometimes, police officers pretend that they want to arrest the "bankers". This is quickly resolved when they receive a small amount of money and disappear with a smile.

On the footpath, on the main road of Alexandria, one can buy expensive cans of butter which are marked "Gift from the American

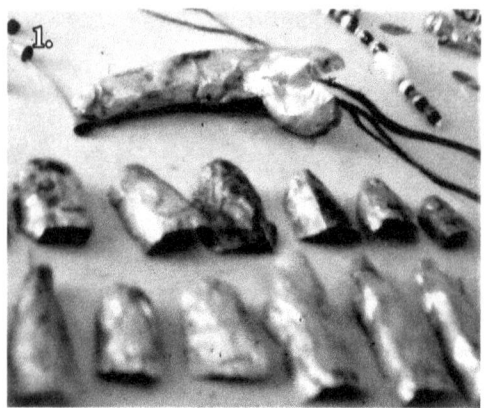

Photo 1: Gold covers for fingers and toes and…
Photo 2: The "Boy King"
Photo 3: Ramesses III, BC 1198
Photo 4: Nedjemet, wife of Herihor

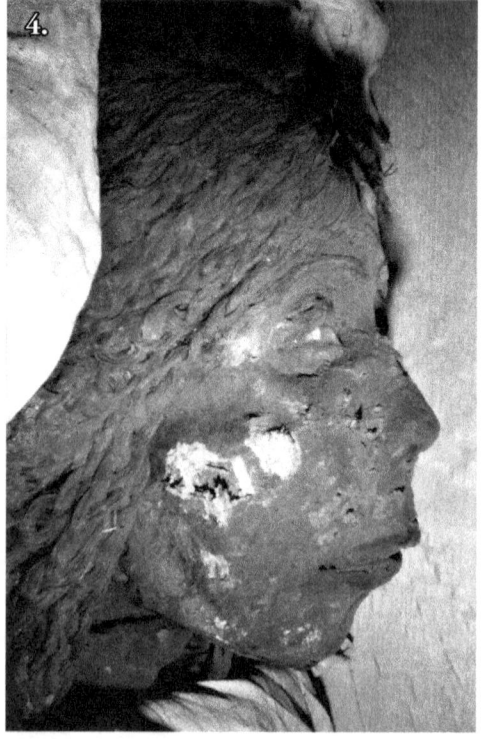

people". In cellars under some houses, there are shelves stacked with imported cans of food and even fresh vegetables. The police ring every now and then and announce their visit. They find empty shelves with a few items as a souvenir for them. No wonder one sees so many police officers around town. *Are their uniforms available on the black market too?*

A fascinating place to visit is the Egyptian Museum. It is well worth spending a whole day there to learn how the ancient Egyptians lived and what they looked like after they died. Every aspect of daily life is depicted on wall paintings and in wood carvings. Everything which has been found in temples and graves has been put in the museum for the benefit of the tourists. Of course, many of the most valuable items have ended up in museums around the world, from London to Paris and Berlin. But there is still enough to be admired here in Cairo.

A special room contains the mummies of the Pharaohs. It is locked, and photography is not permitted. They were kings, after all. I grease the hand of a guard with a few Piaster notes and hide the camera until he looks away.

Call it bribery but, nothing is impossible in Egypt with some *baksheesh*. For instance, alcohol can easily be purchased through back doors and under the counter. In Moslem countries, alcohol is illegal. But Cairo is a very international city—the centre of the Middle East—and is flexible, in many ways. My local and international driver's licence cost me three colour films. I only learn to drive much later in Australia.

The mummies lie in beautiful coffins with glass covers. As shown in these photographs. Note the blue eye of Nedjemet; it is a polished stone. In modern times, it has not yet been possible to produce exactly the same colour. Note also that the braids of the hair are well preserved.

It is said that the brains have been removed through incisions in the nose or openings in the skull, as can be seen on the depression behind the eye of Tuthmosis. A piece of bone has been removed but could not be put back properly. After thousands of years, it is still obvious that he was an intelligent ruler.

Another highlight of the museum is the exhibit of Tut-ankh-Amun, the Boy King. I admire the mask and the spare parts. Gold covers for the fingers and toes and…. Nothing has been forgotten. *I wonder if they would fit me?*

Then, it is Christmas, and for the first time, I am away from home in a distant land. As planned, I attend the service in the Lutheran Church. The congregation sings the German Christmas songs competing with the noise of donkey carts, the hooting of cars, and the call, by loudspeaker, from a Mosque tower nearby for Muslims to come for prayers: *"Allah u Akbar!"*

After the Church service, Axel and I are invited to a home for orphaned children. An old German lady runs it, and the children call her Mum. I get dressed as Father Christmas and distribute little presents to the kids.

In the Youth Hostel, this morning, we were told we may have to move out. A tour group is expected. *Will I end up sleeping in the street, worse than Jesus?* Thankfully, the group seems to find better accommodation.

When we return to the hostel, I find that the rats have stolen some of the food I had hidden in my rucksack. I try to take revenge: I put a banana on the floor, climb onto my bunk bed, hold my scout knife between my fingers, and plan to drop it on a rat. But they are faster than I am. When I turn away for a moment, the banana has disappeared. I find the skin on the stairs the next morning. The hostel manager sets traps when I tell him the story. My big toe almost gets caught in it. The next night, we stick coat hangers in the space under the door to stop the rats from squeezing through. So, the rats have to stay in the bedroom of the girls.

I spend the last days of the year exploring Cairo on foot. I love to stroll along the Nile at night, when it is cooler, and enjoy the roads with less traffic. There are also no beggars to hassle me. Axel takes off to Upper Egypt to visit the ancient temples and the Valley of the Kings.

It is New Year's Eve, and I spend it with Axel and Karl in the hostel. It is a quiet evening. Axel has bought a bottle of brandy and we also have some beer. Of course, it is forbidden to drink alcohol in the hostel. When our drinks are finished, I go to the manager of the hostel and ask him if he can give me some of the "tea" in his can. He fills a glass for me. I am sure that brew contains more alcohol than our brandy! As payment, he asks me for my necktie. No way! I need it for when I will start working in Alexandria.

At midnight, we stumble onto the balcony. Karl, my Canadian mate, is with us. We turn our heads toward Germany and wish each other and our relatives at home a Happy New Year. In a rather drunken hope that our best wishes can be heard in Germany, I take live ammunition from my gas pistol, which has been "doctored," and shoot six signal bullets into the air.

Karl shouts, "The Jews are coming!!! The Jews are coming!!!"

Just as well that Axel does not fire his 9mm pistol with real ammunition and without a license.

My shooting has an unexpected result. On the other side of the road is the American Embassy. A few weeks previously, Congolese students had set fire to the Embassy's library, so, a truckload of Egyptian police now guard the Embassy.

Upon our drunken commotion, the police come running towards the hostel, holding their shields and sticks. Karl runs too … taking my pistol with him into the toilet.

*Sunset in Alexandria, the photo for which
I get arrested as an Israeli spy.*

The hostel manager and a police officer come running up the stairs and demand to know what has happened. I stand straight like a soldier and tell them we only lit a few firecrackers, as is the custom in Germany. The other tramps in the room nod and say "Yes" while they suppress their laughter. The manager and the officer believe the excuse and depart.

It is the start of the New Year in 1965.

It is also the start of my work in Alexandria. The office of Hochtief AG (P/L) is on the ground floor of a building on the Corniche. It is a long and winding road, that hugs the bay of Alexandria from the harbour in the west to the Montazah Palace in the east.

The company has several building contracts: a sewer tunnel under the Nile in Cairo; relocation of the ancient temple of Kalabsha to higher ground to save it from the rising waters of Lake Nasser behind the Aswan High Dam; and they build a dry dock in Alexandria. The Russians use it to repair their warships. Hochtief AG is also in charge of the engineering project during the relocation of the Temple of Abu Simbel in Upper Egypt, an international project of the United Nations.

The accounting for all of these projects is undertaken in Alexandria on a machine that I operate. I also help to compile the monthly reports and balance sheets for the Head office in Essen, Germany. This keeps me busy for the next two and a half years.

Unfortunately, after two weeks, my stomach gets sick, and my eyes turn yellow. I end up in hospital with Hepatitis A and B. In King Fuad II Hospital, there are about twelve German nurses who look after me and spoil me; they probably save my life. After four weeks, I am well enough to return to work. I am grateful to the company that pays for the bed and medical costs and does not sack me.

For the first half of the year, I work for lousy pay and a local contract. But, I still manage to change enough Egyptian pounds on the black market into US dollars to pay for an air ticket to Sudan and Ethiopia. The manager hears about my travel plans and offers me a foreign contract, which I accept. Suddenly, I earn four times as much as in Germany but have to work unlimited overtime for the next two years. The company puts me into a cheap guest house run by an Austrian lady where I can also eat some decent food. My savings account in Berlin grows rapidly while I still live as cheaply as possible in Alexandria. Axel and Karl continue their travels and sadly, I never hear from them again.

After work, sometimes, I end up in the nightclubs, have a beer, and watch the belly dancers and floor shows. When the girls sit next to me and want me to buy them a drink, they only get a coke. When they offer to take me to a back room, I say, *"Mish mumkin. Ana Abu leban."* (Not possible. I am impotent.) They pretend to believe me.

When I have more than one day off, I make excursions. I make a bus trip from Marsamatru, on the west coast, to the Siwa Oasis that is 250 kilometres south. I visit the monasteries in Wadi Natrun in the desert between Alexandria and Cairo.

A special trip with a couple of Franciscan Monks takes me to Jebel Musa (Moses Mountain) and the Saint Catherine's Monastery on the Sinai Peninsula. It is the mountain where God gave the Ten Commandments to Moses.

During this time, the company is building a bridge across the Nile near Qena in Upper Egypt. The Israelis destroy it during the six-day war in 1967. A business trip gives me a chance to hire a bicycle so that I can make an excursion to the temple at Luxor and the Valley of the Kings, including, among others, the grave of Tut-Ankh-Amun. Early in 1967, the war propaganda against Israel begins. By then our office has been moved to Cairo. I now work on the fourteenth floor of the Immobile Building in the city with a view over Cairo. This also permits a view that goes all the way to the pyramids. Completed in 1940, it was the first skyscraper in Cairo and used to be the highest building in the Middle East. But there is little time to look out of the window as I hammer away on my accounting machine.

Nightclub in Cairo, 1.3.1967

During this time, unrest grows in Cairo. Plenty of flags appear in the streets, loudspeakers call for the Holy War against Israel, bus headlights get painted blue, and I stop walking around with my camera. I don't want to be seen as a Jewish spy again. I survived WWII and have no desire to experience another war.

My bank account, by this time, is looking healthy. I am not worried about the Israelis but about the Egyptian mob. It is time to pack my rucksack. The company is considering closing the office and removing the German employees back to Germany.

Sudan, Eritrea, and Ethiopia

I tell the company manager that I do not intend to live in Germany again. So, I give my notice and hop onto a flight bound for Khartoum, the capital of Sudan. There is no time to have a look at Abu Simbel; I could get stuck there. The war begins two days after I leave and ends as a disaster for Egypt after one week.

Heia Safari! I continue my trip to Cape Town.

In Khartoum, I am suddenly in Africa. It is one of the few countries in Africa where the people look almost black and have curly hair. The sun is truly hot here. Everybody is friendly. No one spits like the Egyptians do or scratch their balls quite like them.

I befriend a couple of students, and they show me the way to the "Youth Hostel" on the university grounds. It is a concrete room with a tin roof and a bed in the corner. I stay there for a couple of nights and have a quick look around Khartoum. A warden puts a stamp in my Youth Hostel card. Later on, in India, this will help me to travel as a student at half-price on the trains.

Sudan is also supposed to be at war with Israel. But, I am told that their soldiers hope to arrive on the front when the war is finished. Good luck to them!

It is sad that there is no time to visit the Pyramids of Meroe or travel south by road to Ethiopia. In South Sudan, the population is made up of African tribes who are Christians and want to have their own state independent from the Muslims in the north. Sadly, a small-scale civil war has been going on for years. Tourists travelling through that area risk their lives. The problem is not a religion but the rich oil fields in the south.

Ethiopia is virtually closed to visitors, and so, I need a letter from the German Embassy in Cairo for a visa. Arriving in Asmara, Ethiopia, after Cairo and Khartoum, is a bit of a shock. Asmara is the capital of Eritrea which used to be an Italian colony. It only became attached to Ethiopia in 1952, ever since Eritrea wants to be a separate country. Like in Sudan, a small-scale war has been going on for years.

I manage to catch the last plane to Asmara in Eritrea before the Israelis bomb the airport and destroy the runway! When I get off the plane, I take a deep breath. Asmara lies at an altitude of 2,500m on a plateau. The air is cool and thin. One has to breathe more often to put enough oxygen onto the lungs. I find myself a room in a small guest house and explore the city. European food and cold beer are the first attraction. The second one is the young ladies. They seem to be a mixture between Africans and Arabs and must be the best-looking females in Africa. If it is true that mankind started in Ethiopia, then

Bus to Siwa Oasis, 1.7.1966

Siwa and Agami

Eve must have looked like an Eritrean. I am lucky and manage to befriend one of them. Welcome to Ethiopia!

The next morning I decide to have a look at Massaua, a port city on the Red Sea. It takes the bus 3.5 hours to make its way down a very steep and winding road to the coast. The temperature climbs up from 15ºC to +35ºC. Disappointingly, there is not much to be seen and I only stay for one night before climbing back onto the bus.

A few kilometres before Asmara, an army jeep, with a machine gun mounted on the back, stops the bus. The passengers are forced to get off and are searched. I slowly move to the sand off the road, where I can throw myself behind a rock if the shooting starts. But a soldier stops a car and tells the driver to take me back to Asmara. After this experience, I feel it may be a good idea to move on. *Who knows what can happen on the roads to Addis Ababa?* I buy an air ticket with stopovers on the way.

Axum
10.6.1967

It takes only forty-five minutes to fly to Axum in the province of Tigray next to Eritrea. This city was started some 400 years before

Historic fortification against a British attack in Khartoum

Christ, and it dates back to King Solomon and the Queen of Sheba of the Old Testament.

Axum has a church where the stone plates with the Ten Commandments are supposed to be kept. No access! There are also some stone obelisks dating back 1,700 years before Christ.

About 60% of the population is Christian. Most of the others are Muslims. Churches have books made of leather pages with beautiful paintings and are written in Ge'ez an ancient writing, which can be traced back to the hieroglyphs of Egypt. Hidden

Steles in Axum. They are markers of underground tunnels.

behind curtains are religious paintings, which are fascinating to my European eyes.

The next stop is Gondar, another city with palace ruins. It was founded in the 16th century and is the main city in the Amhara province. I explore the ruins and visit some churches with their beautiful paintings. Since Religion arrived in Ethiopia 400 years before Christ, and is basically the Jewish religion of the Old Testament. Paintings of scenes from the New Testament can be found in the old bibles too.

Photo Top Left: Church painting behind curtain

Photo Bottom Left: God in Gondar

Photo Bottom Right: Killing the dragon

CHAPTER 3:

Further Travels across East Africa

Ethiopia
12. 6. 1967

My flight to Bahir Dar leaves early in the afternoon. The plane is a DC3 from WWII with benches for parachutists along the walls. Stacks of bags and crates are held in place by nets. The pilots ask me to stand between them as we fly along the deep and winding valleys of the Blue Nile; it is an absolute spectacle. They share their drinks and sandwiches with me.

Bahir Dar is the starting point for excursions to the Abbai Falls (Blue Nile Falls.) The town is a port on Lake Tana and the capital city of the Amhara region. Like Asmara in Eritrea, it looks a lot like a European town with wide avenues lined by palm trees.

Lake Tana is the origin of the Blue Nile, and its waterfall is found near Bashir Dar. I spend the rest of the day exploring the city and, the next morning, I take a taxi to the Blue Nile Falls. There has been plenty of rain, and I can admire the falls in all their glory. They are only forty-five metres high. But the thunder of the falling water and

Blue Nile Falls on a cloudy day

the mist rising from the deep are most impressive. Few tourists make it to this part of Ethiopia.

Thankfully, there still is time for a trip by motorboat to the small monastery of Kubran Gabriel on a tiny island in Lake Tana.

My flight to Addis Ababa is booked for the next day. On arrival in a new place, the first task is always to find accommodation. I end up in a small guest house or Bar Buna Bet (Coffee Bar) at Mercato, the market area. It is not one of the best areas of Addis Ababa. Addis lies at an altitude of 2,400 m. Like Asmara, it has cool and fresh air, but with half a million inhabitants, it is a lot bigger and the capital city of Ethiopia. By the way, Ethiopia is a very large country with at least eighty different tribes and many different languages and cultures. Emperor Haile Selassie still rules the country. But he is an old man now and getting frail.

When I walk around, I notice a large construction site and a crane with the company logo of Ph. Holzmann, another big German civil engineering company like Hochtief AG. They are attaching a few new buildings to Haile Selassie University. By now, I have used up a lot of my travel budget. It may be an idea to work again for a while. I meet the site engineer and ask if he needs any help. He advises me that he needs a storekeeper and offers me a local pay and free accommodation in a bachelor home with other German employees. I accept and agree to start work ten days later.

The job of a storekeeper is very different from working on an accounting machine. There are about eighty Ethiopian workers on site. I have to employ more, if necessary, and part of my job is to fill in time cards, pay wages, hand out the tools in the morning, and collect them at night. My store is in a mess and needs organising, and I have to learn the names of all the tools plus nails, et cetera, in Amharic. Most of the workers do not know how to read and write and, they do not understand English. I soon learn a lot of Amharic swear words.

There are four German foremen and soon, I become one of the team and try to get along with the workers, as well. Like in Egypt, I have to work hard for my money. There is plenty of unpaid overtime. After work, I go home, eat, have a shower, and climb on the company bicycle from my store. It takes me all over Addis and its many hills, at

Construction site in Addis Ababa. My store on the right.

Photo 1: Revoval of floor at night
Photo 2: German Ambassador, Haile Selassie, Site Engineer
Photo 3: Emperor Haile Selassie and his dog

night. The Ethiopians in the dance bars in the suburbs start laughing when they see a foreigner *(Ferengi)* parking his bike between their cars.

Sometimes they buy me a beer, point to the bar, and say, "Try this girl or that one."

No more comments on this subject!

My colleagues take the minibus when they go out. They drink too much and end up in fights with the Ethiopians. One of them gets arrested, and I have to talk very nicely to an Army Officer to get him out of jail. As compensation, the officer gets the free use of one of our cars for the next day.

One day, a screw of the concrete mixer has become loose; it was not properly assembled. As a result, a whole floor of a building gets poured full of concrete which never sets. Our purchase officer buys all the pickaxes he can find in town, and I spend a night supervising the workers who have to clean up the mess.

It is a DM 40.000 mistake which could cost the site engineer his job if the Head Office were to find out as the German Government finances the project.

One day, Emperor Haile Selassie visits the site and has a look around my store.

He shakes my hand, and I respectfully bend down low and say, "Welcome to my store, your Majesty."

He answers, "It is all very neatly arranged," and climbs up the stairs of one of the new buildings. His bodyguard soldiers point their submachine guns at the workers.

On another day, one of the workers falls into a cellar where a large brick falls on him and breaks his leg. They carry him into my store, and, in horror, I see a bone below the knee sticking out. I quickly stabilise the leg with a couple of boards. We take him to the hospital in our minibus and carry him all the way to the operating table.

My store

A few months later, he appears at my window with a walking stick and thanks me for saving his life.

When the roof on top of one of the buildings has been completed, there is a party. Goats from my store get slaughtered. Every worker gets a morsel.

I give a speech: "You build this university, and you earn very little money. But one day, your sons may study here and provide for you in your old age. Hence, you are working for the future of your country."

Sometimes, I have a weekend off. I use it for excursions on public buses to surrounding areas like Lake Langano or, to take part in the celebrations of the Meskel feast. It is the day on which—according to legend—the Queen of Sheba found the true cross on which Jesus was crucified. There is a parade in the city and, at Meskel Square, people march around a huge fire.

A few weeks after I started work here, another tramp appears at my store window and asks me for a job. He is Max Gallmann from Switzerland. I take him to the site engineer. He is a draughtsman and gets a job at Holetta, a small town about forty kilometres from Addis.

At weekends, he visits us in Addis and joins us when we explore the nightclubs.

Max too, wrote a report about his trip to Ethiopia. I have translated it and include it here in my tales:

(Zürich, July-August 1967: My Trip to Africa by Max Gallmann)
Sali alle miteinand! (Greetings to all!)

I am Max Gallmann from Switzerland and will put some of my travel experiences in writing.

Switzerland is a rather beautiful country in the centre of Europe. Her mountains are great for climbing, and the mountain meadows invite you to try some yodelling. I had finished school and an apprenticeship and served in the army. My friend, Hans Greuter, at 26 years, was of the same age as I, and he was driving earth-moving machines on construction sites.

We both liked to swim and dive. The mountain lakes in Switzerland are a bit cold and have no coral reefs and colourful fish. That made us long for a holiday in Southern Italy. After a bit of planning, we quit our jobs and packed our luggage and diving gear into my old Ford Transit bus.

We said goodbye to our parents at the end of July 1967 and took off. We needed only four days to travel the 1,500 kilometres to the south of Italy. On the first day, we made it to Terrocina, on the west coast of Italy between Rome and Naples. The next day was an adventurous drive through mountainous and romantic Calabria until we reached Reggio di Calabria, at the southern tip of Italy.

From there, we took a car ferry to Messina on the island of Sicily. Along the north coast, we drove to Palermo, the capital city of Sicily. After a rest, we continued on a scenic road along the Mediterranean Sea to Trapani, where we slept on the beach. Overnight, my sandals were stolen. I continued barefoot.

Photo 1: An Islander and Hans in our rubber dinghy.

Photo 2: Pantelleria, Scauri basso. Hans is filling scuba diving tanks with our elf-made compressor unit, driven by a Lambretta scooter engine.

Photo 3: My Ford Transit bus on the wharf at Trapani

Photo Below: The arrival of Werner and Jürgen on board of "Aurora"

From Trapani, a ferry carried us to the smaller island of Pantelleria. This was our destination. The voyage took six hours over a rough sea. Many passengers became seasick.

After arrival, the friendly local people invited us for an octopus stew on the harbour jetty and gave us a small box of shrimps as a thank you for freeing an entangled fishing net from the screw of a fish cutter.

We spent a happy week snorkelling and diving among the red coral reefs, admired the colourful fish, and slept in our sleeping bags on the rocky shore. The rocks were warm after the sun shone on them all day.

The coffee and the traditional wine were very tasty and stopped us from drying out. We were in no hurry to return to Switzerland.

I had no idea that soon, I would experience a change of life, a chain of events and adventures that would alter my future forever.

We met two German globetrotters by the names of Werner and Jűrgen. They had bought a fishing boat in Genoa and explored the Mediterranean Sea, catching fish and selling it to make a living. They had a bit of bad luck in Palermo, where a lot of their belongings were stolen.

Hans and I could not resist asking them if we could join them on one of their fishing trips. They did not mind at all. After eight months in their boat, they became a bit bored with each other and longed for other company.

We left our minibus with a friend in Pantelleria, put our diving gear and clothes into the boat, towed a rubber dingy behind, and off we were on the way to Tunis in Tunisia in North Africa. Without a compass or any other nautical instruments, we had to navigate by the movements of the sun. That was rather unreliable, and we missed Cape Bon in Tunisia. Worse was that the waves were getting higher by the hour until a storm made our boat dance up and down. Hans did not hold on to the edge of the boat properly and suddenly was thrown overboard. He had swallowed some water by the time we rescued him.

In the meantime, the storm continued unabated. The wind-beaten waves had white foam caps and may have reached at least a height of four metres. There was no visibility because the air was full of water spray. Our boat took on water. Waves swept over the sides. The man at the helm had the exhausting job of trying to steer the boat head-on into a wave and to avoid being hit side-on. But, it happened anyhow, and the boat was carried to the crest of a wave, on a precarious angle. We did not know if it was going to turn over or not, and we almost stopped breathing for a few seconds while staring into the watery abyss below. Werner and Hans were frantically scooping water from the bottom of the boat with our cooking pots and tossing the accumulating water overboard while I searched for more containers.

Then, a big wave rocked the boat, and I was thrown into the hold, sustaining a gashing wound on my leg. Exhausted, Jürgen left the helm and curled up astern, face down, while Werner took over. The situation became desperate, and I prayed to God with tears in my eyes. It could have been a scene from the TV series "Air Crash Investigation" where survivors talked about their emotional state while facing death. Thankfully, by late afternoon, the storm started to calm down a bit.

After ten hours though, we still did not see any land. I figured out that we had been pushed south by the storm and were drifting parallel to the coast at a distance of about thirty kilometres. After some arguing, we changed course, and steered west towards the sunset. Three hours passed before we saw flickering lights appear in the dusk. Land at last! There were coral reefs and rocks in the water, which made landing a bit tricky. Exhausted, we stumbled up onto one of the jetties from the shore.

Two coast guards greeted us and demanded answers to their question: "Where did you come from?"

Cape Bon, Tunisia

When we pointed at our boat and replied, "From Pantelleria," they looked at us in disbelief.

"It must be your luckiest day. We never go out with our coast patrol ships in stormy weather like this."

Nearby was a restaurant. The kitchen opened for us during the night. The owner told us that we were close to Nabeul and that it would be wise to travel to Tunis to obtain visitor visas. However, he contacted the Customs Authority. They arrived within the hour when we were in the middle of the dining.

They calmly established their makeshift office in the restaurant and put their mobile office desk right next to our table, stamping pads and stamps all neatly lined up on it.

Then, we had to present ourselves, one by one, to the Customs Officials for identification. Hans and I did not even have a passport, only a Swiss Identification card. They presented us with temporary visas and told us to get passports at the Swiss Consulate in Tunis and then obtain visas from the Tunisian Customs Bureau. Hans and I had originally not intended to travel any further than Pantelleria and were therefore not prepared at all for such an unexpected adventure.

Werner and Jürgen were in possession of German passports but still had to obtain Tunisian visas.

The next morning we made our way north and before rounding Cape Bon on the way to Tunis, where we had a rest in the small town of Kelibia. The locals seemed to like us.

Everybody brought some food for us: figs, cactus fruit, fried corn cobs, bread, milk, and a lamp to help us see what we ate in the darkness before sunrise. Luxury was a washing bowl full of the national dish, couscous, a mixture of a pudding made from crushed wheat with peas, pepperoni, and hot spices.

Later on, we tried some fishing. But only five small fish got caught in our net.

We decided to stay for the night in the friendly place and rolled our sleeping bags out on the rocks near the beach, which were still warm after a sun-drenched day.

Early the next morning, a local holidaymaker joined us in Kelibia for the boat trip to Tunis.

Mustapha, whom we met on Pantelleria, was very useful in helping us to obtain the permit for the stay in the harbour of Tunis. There he left us and went to his home in town.

A visit to the Libyan consulate followed. We needed visitor visas for our next destination on the way to Ethiopia. I was still not

On the way to Tunis. From left: Werner, Hans, Jürgen and Mustafa

Photo Above: Arrival in the harbour of Tunis

Photo Right: Street scene in Kelibia

homesick. After completing our legal obligations in Tunis, we retraced our steps around Cape Bon, then all the way south, passing Sousse, Madias, Sfax, the island of Djerba (Houmt Souk), and Zarzis.

We passed Zarzis about 300 m parallel to the coast when suddenly a guy came running out from his Customs House brandishing his revolver and wildly gesticulating with his arms in the air while screaming at the top of his voice. His confusing hand signals seemed to indicate that he wanted us to come ashore. So, we did. We surrendered our passports to him and were made prisoners on the flat rooftop of the Customs House for the night. At least we did not get hungry, as we were fed with fresh bread and grapes. The next morning, he allowed us off the roof and told us our passports were in order. Before he let us go, we had to admire and pat his flock of camels in the backyard. It was obviously his hobby in this lonely outpost. Arresting us had made his day.

As we continued our journey along the coast, we had to battle through shallow water and, after shearing the pin of the propeller, had to push the boat for a while. We managed to insert another pin into the propeller hub and, through the propeller shaft, reached deeper water and finally arrived in Tripoli, the capital of Libya.

Tripoli, 27.8.1967
On the wharf, a police officer was waiting with the pistol in hand, pointing it at us.

"Where do you come from?" he asked.

"From that boat down there," we replied.

The tide was low, and one could not see the boat from above the wharf. Carefully the officer walked towards the edge while keeping a safe distance from us and looked down to confirm the existence of the boat.

"And now, you guys, get behind one another, form a single file, and I will give the marching orders!" he shouted. At a safe distance, he walked behind us still with pistol in hand, shouting, "Right, left, and straight ahead."

After a few hundred yards of walking through piles of stored goods, we arrived at the Harbour Police Station. Everything worked out all right. Our papers were in order. They even apologised for the rough welcome we had received. We were told it would be unwise to continue our trip because at this time of the year, the storms make the travel very unsafe.

"It was a miracle that you survived the voyage from Pantelleria to Tripoli," said the Officer in Charge.

After checking our passports, the Immigration Officer let us roll out our sleeping bags on the jetty. It became our home where we washed and repaired our clothes and prepared for the next stage of our trip. The Police and Immigration Officers became quite friendly and invited us for coffee. A small shop nearby provided us with basic food. None of us had much money for the trip by boat to Egypt.

Werner was anxious to get to his parents in Addis Ababa. He told Hans and me that his parents might offer us jobs. We decided to ask the Harbour Master if he wants to buy the fishing boat and the rubber dingy. After some haggling over the price, he agreed to buy the boats and our equipment. We shared the money from the sale. Jürgen took his share and made his own plans. The next day, Hans and I bought our air tickets to Asmara in Ethiopia. A direct flight did not exist. We had to obtain visas for Egypt and Sudan.

Tripoli, 30.8.1967

It has been four weeks since our departure from Switzerland. In the evening, the four of us boarded a flight on Air Algerie and flew to Cairo, where we had to change planes. Because there was no flight to Khartoum available on this day, the airline provided us with rooms at the Airport Hotel. After sleeping rough under the open sky for four weeks, we enjoyed the hot showers and comfortable beds. The next morning, we went to Cairo to confirm our flights to Khartoum in Sudan.

We felt a bit out of place. No foreigner could be seen in the streets. Hotels and public buildings, even restaurants, were covered with boards. The entrances were blocked by sandbags. Cars had their headlights covered with rags with little slits in the middle. The headlights of buses were painted with blue paint. The six-day war with Israel from 5 June to 10 June 1967 had just finished. It was not a time for a holiday in Egypt.

The next day a Fokker Friendship of Sudan Airways took us to Khartoum with a stopover in Port Sudan. The welcome by the guards at the airport was disappointing. They did not want us to leave the airport because we had no vaccination passes. Just on time, an African businessman who spoke German asked us what the problem was? He started a lively discussion with the guards, who took fifteen minutes. Afterwards, we were permitted to leave the airport. The following day, the Swiss consul in Khartoum could hardly believe our story. He told us that normally visitors without vaccination passes must return to their home countries. Well, I guess we are not normal.

Finding a place to sleep was the next problem. The sheiks, ministers, and kings of the Arabic countries were attending a conference in Khartoum. Twice, we saw President Nasser of Egypt when he passed us in his Cadillac. We were told that only Hotel Royal had a vacant room for us. I almost fainted when I heard the name of the hotel. We barely managed to find enough money to pay for ten days. With only 30,000 Lira on us and a miserable exchange rate, there was no money left for food.

We stood in front of the hotel entrance and stared at the name: Hotel Royal & Garden. Well, inside, it looked more like the yard of a scrap merchant. Bathtubs had been turned upside down, and discarded rusty bed frames decorated the rooms. Chairs were broken, tables dirty, and iron pipes had been torn from the walls. At the entrance, the receptionist, an Arab in Khaki shorts and a grubby singlet, sat at an old teacher's desk covered with flies. He expressed his delight in the fact that distinguished German and Swiss travellers had found their way to his hotel.

On entering a room with four beds, we were greeted by a swarm of flies with inexhaustible agility. They stayed with us for the next ten days and entertained us with their acrobatics. The beds had been imported from the nearby hospital. They still had mattresses and were covered with almost clean bed sheets. Judging by the colour they had not been used more than three times. The ceilings were covered with spider webs, and motorised breadcrumbs crawled on the floor. It is impossible to describe the smell of the place. I think it was the smell of the great wide world.

But, we experienced a special luxury. A loudspeaker, mounted in a wooden box, had been placed in the garden. Every night, some Sudanese people had a party, ate a lot, and played the music of the Orient on an old gramophone. Maybe they obtained it when a radio station was liquidated. Sometimes, the needle got stuck in the record, and the same sound was repeated over and over, or the motor operated at different speeds. Perhaps this happened to the gramophone due to dirt on the record. By international standards, the hotel was cheap. But soon, we were broke. I had no choice but to pay the Swiss consul a visit and was able to sell him my watch for ten pounds. Now, we had enough money for the visas for Ethiopia. But we still had no onward ticket as proof that we would leave Ethiopia again.

So, we booked a flight via Asmara in Eritrea to Djibouti, a French territory.

We obtained tourist visas from the French consulate. We also went for vaccinations against Yellow Fever and Smallpox in order to obtain the vaccination pass. There was only one flight to Asmara once a week and only one day per week for vaccinations. That explains why we had to spend so much time in Khartoum.

Our money was finished, and our stomachs were empty, very empty. It was our good luck that we met an African from the tribe of the Crocodile People. He had studied physics in Basle, Switzerland. He bought some beer and sandwiches for us and paid half the hotel bill. We were grateful for any donations. Hans already had started vomiting because of hunger and drinking too much water. I managed to catch a cold that lasted for two days. My nose was dripping like a water tap at 45oC in the shade.

An Ethiopian taxi. Herbert Merker is on the left with Hans Greuter and the driver.

Jürgen left us in Khartoum. Hans, Werner, and I continued the trip on our own. Once we had the Ethiopian visas, we visited the Swiss Consul again. He had told us several times that the consulate was no flea market. But he still bought the firelighter from Werner for 2.5 pounds and added another half a pound because he could see how hungry we were. Now, we could afford to buy a few bread rolls to satisfy our hunger.

It was a Sunday morning at 2 am when we finally shouldered our bags and started walking the four kilometres to the airport. Suddenly, a black Ford Zodiac limousine stopped beside us. In it were an African driver and a white passenger. He offered to take us to the airport, telling us he was the Chief Judge of Khartoum. He was blind drunk and passed his bottle of sherry around. From the glove box, he retrieved some sandwiches, which we gratefully devoured.

At Khartoum airport that morning, there was another hiccup. We had overstayed our seven-day visitor visa and were supposed to pay an additional six pounds. But we had just paid for the departure tax and were broke again. The officer at the departure gate felt sorry for us. He told us he would make an exception and pay the fee from his own pocket. Then, he stamped our passports. We pretended that we believed him and said thank you. At 4 am, we finally boarded a Comet plane of Arab Airlines.

During the flight to Asmara, we enjoyed a sumptuous meal and arrived in Ethiopia with contented smiles. It was here that Werner left Hans and me. His parents had sent him an air ticket while we stayed in Khartoum, so he could fly from there to Addis Ababa via Asmara.

Hans and I stayed in Khartoum for another few days, waiting for our cheaper flight to Asmara. Werner promised to wait for us in Addis Ababa.

Hans and I climbed into a bus headed for Asmara. On the bus, we met an American language teacher who was based in Saudi Arabia but spent his holidays in Asmara. His name was Herbert Merker. He spoke German, and during our stay in Asmara, he proved to be a good friend. He spent 235 dollars on us, which we promised to pay back as soon as we have a job.

Our bus stopped for a toilet break on the way to Addis Ababa

Asmara is a beautiful little town at about 2,300 m above sea level and has very many beautiful and dark brown young ladies. What a lovely welcome to Ethiopia!

After a few days, it was time to travel to Addis Ababa. The trip in a crowded bus, which made us feel like sardines, took three days. There were many stops on the way.

The Fiat Diesel motor had its weaknesses and had to be repaired by the driver and the passengers during the trip. Hungry and dirty, we finally reached Addis Ababa, the capital of Ethiopia, where Werner was waiting for us. After a few days, I found a lowly paid job as a draughtsman with the German Civil Engineering company of Ph. Holzmann on a construction site in Holetta, forty kilometres from Addis Ababa.

They were extending the Technical University in Addis that was being paid for by the German Government. In Holetta, they built a school in a military compound. Hans found work with a Swiss roofing contractor in Addis.

In Addis, they had a storekeeper by the name of Manfred Richter. Like me, he had arrived a few weeks previously and was working to save some money for his trip to Cape Town, South Africa. We discussed his plans, which I found very attractive. We both saved only a little money. The sinful life in the bars of Addis was too tempting after the long and frugal trip from Europe.

I used to travel between Holetta and Addis Ababa on usually very crowded busses. Once on the way back to Holetta, a passenger next to me moved aside and offered his spot to a lady so she could hold on to a vertical rail.

I said, "You are a gentleman."

He replied, "No, I am brown and poor and wear shabby clothes. You are white with a safari suit and blond hair."

I explained to him in all detail the meaning of being a gentleman. Our conversation got translated into Amharic for all other passengers

Real "Lion of Judah" during Meskel feast; and in the Zoo

Manfred travelled via Spain and Portugal to Morocco in North Africa. I took the shortcut through Italy.

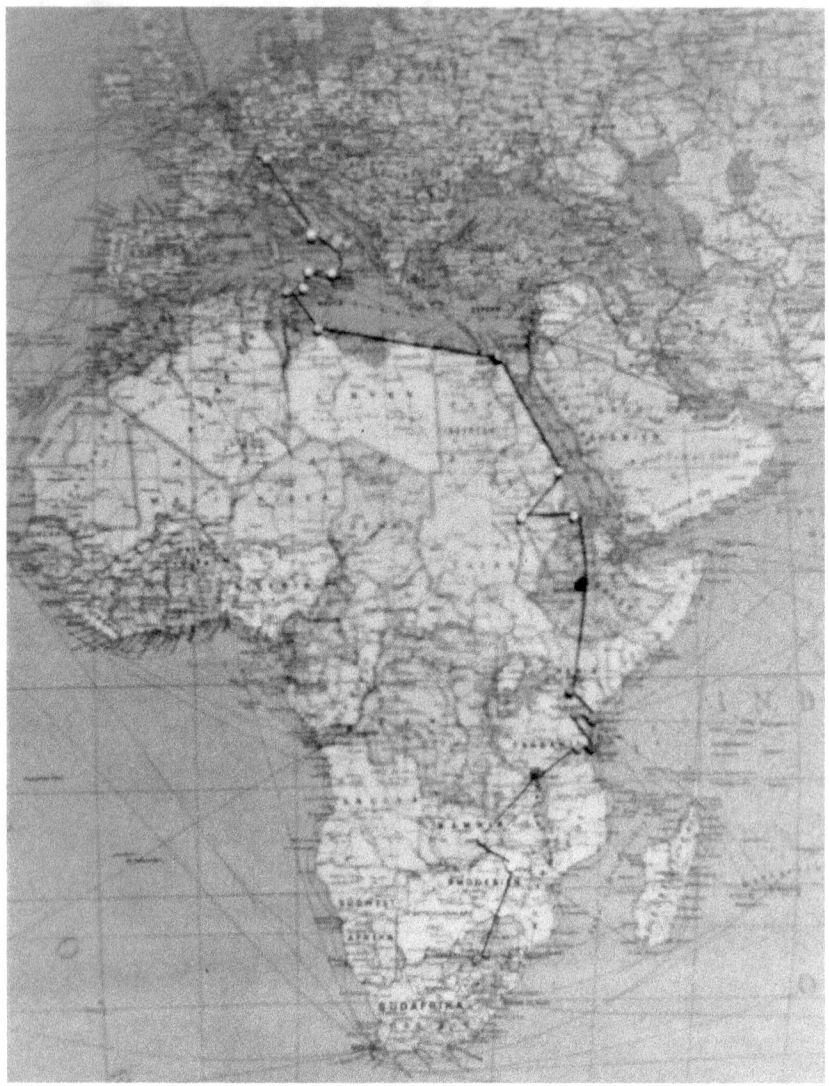

From Libya to South Africa

to understand. One of them noticed a thief who tried to open the pocket of my safari suit where my wallet was. He told the driver to stop the bus. Two strong fellows dragged the offender from the bus, threw him on the ground, and pelted him with stones. They left the bleeding thief lying in the dirt, climbed back into the bus, and we continued our trip. I watched the scene with mixed feelings.

Maybe some of the passengers were Muslims, and I watched the practical application of Sharia Law.

At the time, there was a lot of political tension with the province of Eritrea, which wanted to secede from Ethiopia. It was advisable to leave the country because of the threat of civil war. One day, Emperor Haile Selassie visited the site. He was deposed soon after our departure and died under mysterious circumstances; a sad end for the "Lion of Judah" with a family tree going back to the Queen of Shaba and King Solomon of the Old Testament.

Manfred writes:
Max keeps working for a few more days whereas I leave the job on the 14th December 1967, and plan to have a look at the holy city of Lalibela and also, visit the ancient city of Harrar.

The plane to Lalibela leaves early in the morning on the next day. It is a distance of thirteen kilometres from the airport uphill to Lalibela. I do not climb into the jeep, which is taking passengers but prefers to walk with the Ethiopians but, I send my rucksack on to a hotel. It is a tough climb but, it gives me a chance to enjoy the landscape.

At the entrance of Lalibela, there is a cheap little guest house. I decide to sleep there for a few hours on a bag filled with straw. Unfortunately, some fleas share the bag with me, and they take an interest in me. When I wake up from my sleep, I am itchy all over … The manageress is happy to receive a few dollars from me for the accommodation.

During my travels, I find out that in the 12th century, King Lalibela ruled Ethiopia. At the time, the Muslims had occupied Jerusalem, and pilgrimages to the Holy Land had stopped. The King decided to build a new Jerusalem in Ethiopia and make it his headquarters; he encouraged his people to make pilgrimages to it. With tremendous effort and copper chisels, twelve large stone blocks

Photo Left: House and storage containers in Lalibela
Photo Right: Manageress of Guest House

were cut in the ground and hollowed out to serve as churches. It has become one of the wonders of the world.

There are annual festivals here, and religious pilgrims come to stay for a while and meditate.

My rucksack is waiting for me in the Seven Olives Hotel that has proper beds and no fleas. I spend the next day walking around town and visit with priests who show me around the churches and let me take photos of some pages of their holy books.

For the next day, I hire a mule and a guide and make a tour to a church in a mountain cave at the end of a treacherous trail along a mountainside. It is a tough climb up and down the mountains. At one stage, I get off the mule and hold on to its tail. One wrong step and I could fall into a deep ravine. This part of Ethiopia is known for its mountainous territory. The church is well worth the visit.

I have an early sleep after my excursion and book my flight back to Addis Ababa for the next morning.

Church cut from rock and hollowed out

Ancient book with leather pages and beautiful paintings in Lalibela church

Photo Below: Reading the Bible at Lalibela
Photo Right: Cave dweller with Bible

1.

3.

2.

4.

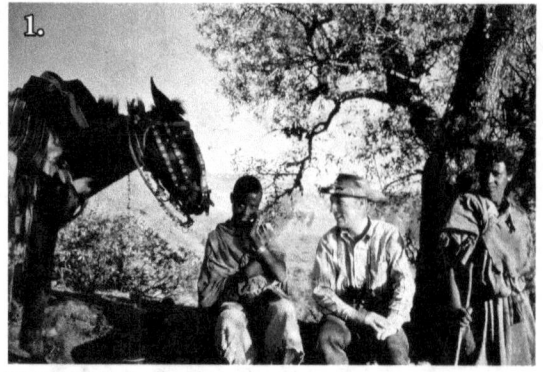

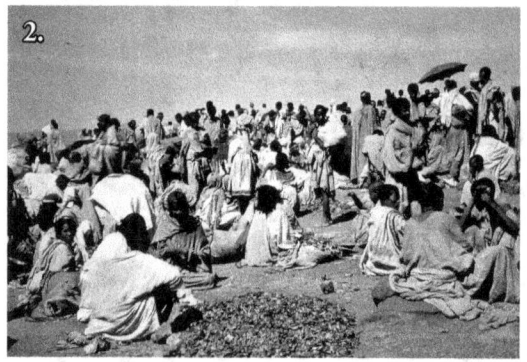

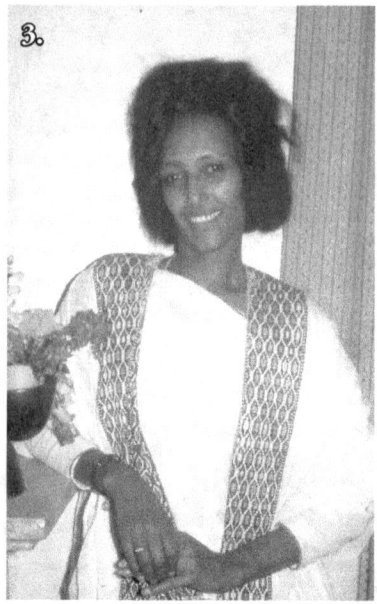

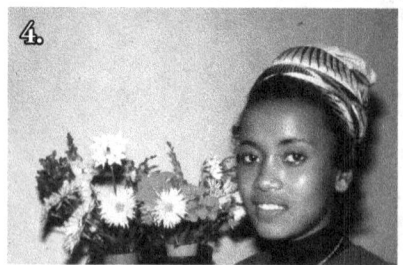

Photo 1: Friendly meeting

Photo 2: Lalibela market

Photos 3 & 4: Will they remember me?

Photo Below: Excursion in Tigray province on mule

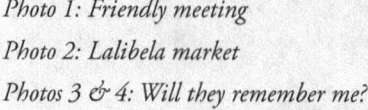

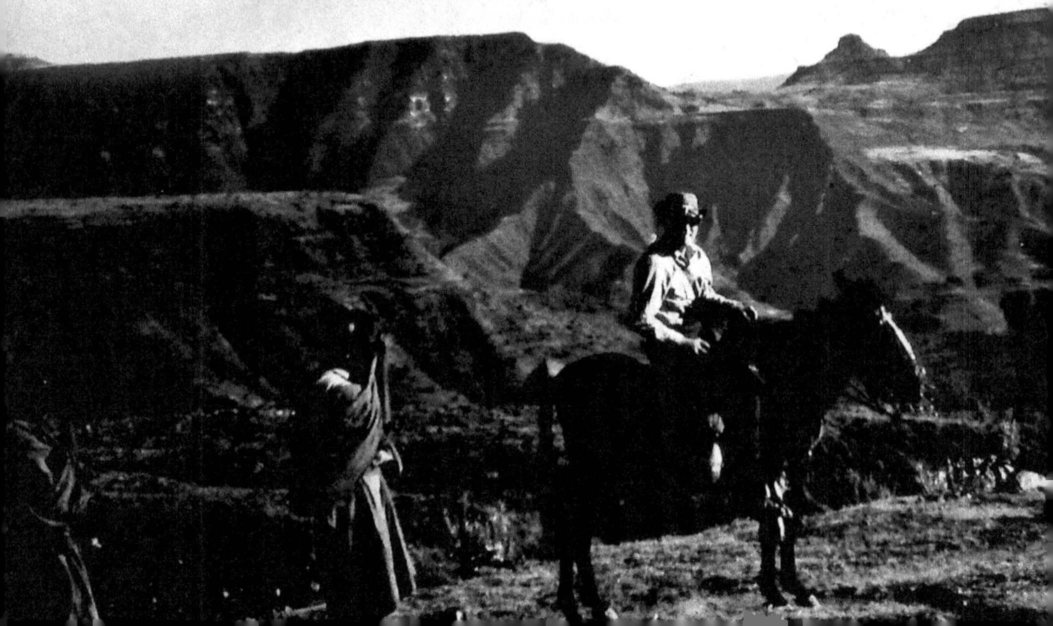

On 20 December, I take a train to Harar. A fellow there feeds wild hyenas with pieces of meat. I plan to join him. Unfortunately, a train door hits my left hand on the way and breaks a finger. I get off the train at a bush hospital and find a nurse who takes a piece of twine from her handbag and stitches the bleeding wound. I have to return to Addis and can only dream of the hungry hyenas.

Christmas, 24.12.1967
Max and I say "Goodbye" to our German colleagues. They wish us good luck. Heia Safari! We are ready for some more adventures and are on our way to Cape Town.

Max and Manfred near Nairobi

CHAPTER 4:

Kenya

The flight of Ethiopian Airlines leaves in the morning. After one and a half hours, we land near Nairobi, the capital of Kenya. We have no tourist visas and no onward tickets. Max has only a few dollars, and I have some travellers' cheques. The police want to put us back on the plane. I explain that single tourists with a lot of money can easily be attacked and robbed. Ethiopian Airlines gives a financial guarantee. We find free accommodation in the Sikh Temple in Nairobi.

Nairobi
24.12.1967
Once we have settled into the Sikh Temple in Nairobi, we ask where the German Lutheran Church is and attend the Christmas service there. It reminds me of the church in Cairo. But this time, we do not get invited afterwards to celebrate. So, there is still time left to explore the city. However, I start feeling pain in my broken finger. I think it is becoming infected after the unprofessional treatment in Ethiopia.

German Church in the background

After having worked in Addis Ababa, it is time to relax for a couple of weeks before we head for Mt.Kilimanjaro in Tanganyika. We will forever be grateful to the Sikhs for the free accommodation. It is part of their religious duties to accommodate travellers irrespective of their ethnicity or religion. I admire them for their tolerance and generosity.

We decide to visit a National Park near Nairobi. For the first time, we see African animals in the wild. We are lucky that a tourist gives us a lift around the park in his car as we have been warned that walking around here could be fatal. Hungry lions or cheetahs could attack humans on foot. There are crocodiles as well in and around the creeks.

Like in Addis, there are plenty of bars here where we learn some African dancing. The girls, in their colourful miniskirts, like to wiggle their 'behinds' around for fun when they are dancing to that very lively and loud African music. It makes us fall in love with Africa.

I decide to attend an Indian private clinic, and my swollen finger gets treated and bandaged properly. I hope it will start healing before I attempt to climb Africa's highest mountain.

On the first day of the New Year, in 1968, we visit the National Museum and enjoy a concert in a park.

9.1.1968

Near Nairobi, a dust road leads to Moshi in Tanzania. The distance to Voi, the nearest bigger town, is 320 kilometres. Our plan for today is to reach Mt.Kilimanjaro with its ice-capped top.

We place our bags under a tree by the side of the road and wait for cars that will take us to our destination. The result is disappointing. Within two hours, only a handful of cars pass us. Their drivers ignore us or only lift their hands, as a greeting. We are getting thirsty and impatient and prepare to march back to Nairobi.

Suddenly, a column of limousines appears. One of them is a Mercedes 600. At the open window sits Jomo Kenyatta, the "Burning Spear"; the hero of Kenya's struggle for independence and now its president. I know that there would be no room in his car next to his bodyguards so, I only take my hat off and bend forward as a respectful greeting. Further, it is forbidden to take photos of Jomo.

Nairobi National Park

After this frustrating experience, we give up and take the next bus which comes along. The fare is cheap. That is why it takes five hours to travel to Moshi. This is partly due to the bad road but also that every tree and every hut along the road seems to be a stop. At one mud-brick hut, the driver stops for half an hour to down a few beers. Afterwards, he does not drive better, but faster.

We pass the southern end of Tsavo National Park. Ostriches and antelopes can be seen by the road appearing to wait for tourists to take photos of them. Finally, we notice a large bank of clouds above the otherwise flat landscape on the right side of the bus. A slope appears and stretches over many kilometres; it is the foot of Mt Kilimanjaro. My second goal in Africa, after the Cheops Pyramid, is coming closer.

Just before the border with Tanzania, we pass a hill that is covered with graves. During WWI, the German General von Lettow-Vorbeck and his Askari-Soldiers fought it out with the British in this location. The graves are a sad souvenir which foreign invaders have left on Africa's soil.

Formalities at the border are simple. Tanzania, by the way, is a combination of Tanganyika and Zanzibar, an island off the coast for which the Germans obtained control from the British. In the days of Lettow-Vorbeck it was called *"Deutsch-Ostafrika"*.

Late in the afternoon, we reach the small town of Moshi. First, we head for a restaurant and order rice with mutton and curry and a large bottle of Tusker Beer. Afterwards, I pay a visit to the local Sikh Temple in order to find accommodation for the next week. Staying in the Temple is for free. But donations will be accepted. I wear the Sikh ring on my wrist as a symbol of international friendship. When I arrive at the temple, a group of ladies stop their singing and praying and ask me to return later when the priest is present. They stick a handful of sweet pudding in my mouth; this is symbolic, like the sharing of bread by Christ. After sunset, Max and I return. The priest

Kilimanjaro, Kibo summit, Postcard

Mawenzi Summit, 13.1.1968

welcomes us. He is a short and friendly old man with his hair in a knot, a long beard, and a white shirt hanging over white trousers.

We are shown into a clean room with mattresses on steel frames and thin blankets. We enter our details in a guest book and receive a lock and keys. Once more, we feel safe and welcome in a strange environment. Nevertheless, it is hard to fall asleep. Max turns the light on, grabs a towel, and kills plenty of mosquitoes on the walls.

Moshi
10.01.1968
After a long sleep, we start our preparation for climbing the mountain. In the distance, far above the clouds, one can see the glaciers on the summit of Mt Kilimanjaro reflecting the morning sun.

Our map shows Uhuru-Peak, formerly known as *"Kaiser Wilhelm Spitze",* with a height of 19,340 feet that equates to about 5,895 metres. Moshi is about 2,000 metres above sea level. All in all, this means that we have to climb about 4,000 metres.

One does not have to be an experienced climber to get to the top of Kibo, which is a volcanic mountain top with an extinct crater in the middle. But many climbers give up because of mountain sickness. Some have died due to heart failure or because of falling asleep while climbing. Uhuru Peak is the highest point of Kibo.

A second mountain top called Mawenzi rises about fifteen kilometres from Kibo. Mawenzi is also a dangerous mountain top to climb and has a height of 5,150 metres. Only recently, two mountaineers from Great Britain died there. The section known as "The Saddle" between Kibo and Mawenzi is at an altitude of about 5,000 metres. It is flat and is a bit higher on both sides; therefore, it is called the "Saddle".

Upon the Saddle, the air is very thin. It makes the last 870 metres, up a steep slope of lava sand, a challenge for any climber who attempts to get to the top of Kibo.

Between the glaciers is a rocky area with a small flagpole called "Gillman's Point". From there, it takes another hour or so of climbing over snow and ice to get to Uhuru Peak, which is sixty metres higher.

We have no idea how far we will get. It is illegal to climb without a guide and porters. One can get arrested but, our budget has no provision for the luxury of climbing in a group with porters. Like climbing Cheops Pyramid, this will be a true adventure, the toughest of our lives.

Prior to climbing, though, we visit Kibo Hotel, at the foot of the mountain, to get some more information about climbing the mountain. A friendly German lady runs the place. But her smile freezes when she hears of our plans. She warns us of any possible mishaps and tells us stories of victims of bad weather and thin air or, of people who got lost in the fog and became fodder for the lions. Max looks worried but starts smiling again when we are shown the price list of guided tours. We say *"Auf Wiedersehen"* and return to Moshi, where we ask for advice from people who are not involved in the tourist business.

Max on the "Saddle". Gillman's Point on top, in the centre

We already have a compass. So, we buy a reliable-looking map of the mountain and the tracks, buy water containers and canned food, and place those items and our warm clothes into my rucksack.

Hat, sunglasses, sun cream, sleeping bags, and photo gear complete our equipment. My rucksack must weigh at least 30 kg. In the evening, we drink a couple of bottles of beer in order to firm our resolve.

Climbing Kilimanjaro
11.01.1968

Yesterday, we were at Kibo Hotel. Today, we make our way back at midday. Two mountaineers from Austria give us a lift in their Volkswagen from Moshi to the Kibo Hotel. A sealed narrow road gently winds its way up the hill. Max carries the rucksack, and I carry the lighter photo bag. Every hour we take turns and, it is the guy with the rucksack who determines the walking speed. We purposely walk slowly to conserve energy. Today's destination is Mandara Hut, formerly *"Bismarck Hütte"* that is located at about 3,000 m altitude. It is some twenty kilometres from Kibo Hotel. We have six hours in which to travel that distance until sunset.

The lower reaches of Kilimanjaro are covered with dense rain forests and, in between, are plantations of bananas, sisal, corn, and coffee. We move through this landscape at a slow pace, sweating and with aching shoulders due to the weight of the rucksack. Every hour, we rest for a while and have a sip of lemon water from our bottles.

Soon, the sealed road turns into a dirt track. During the dry period, it can still be used by Land Rovers. We are exhausted when we finally reach Mandara Hut after just over five hours. An aching back and shaky knees are the results of our effort.

The hut is a simple wooden house with a flat roof and three rooms; the room in the middle has a fireplace. A table, two wooden benches and several double bunks complete the furniture.

Highest hut on Kibo

Max carries the rucksack

Max at Mandara Hut

On the beds, there are mattresses without sheets. The colour and general condition of them gives an idea of the number of visitors. The walls and all wooden surfaces are covered with autographs of previous visitors. Nearby is a shed for the tour guides and porters.

The toilet is very basic indeed. A small creek with clear water emerges from the rain forest and serves as a kitchen, bar, and bathroom. We are already above the lower layer of clouds. As the sun sets, it turns the clouds pink. As the shades of the night slowly cover the savannah, the lights of Moshi and the rising stars provide an African fireworks display.

12.01.68

We sleep well after yesterday's exercise. The dry heat of the steppe has stopped and, at 3,000 metres, one can crawl into a sleeping bag and enjoy the warmth.

A cool morning breeze encourages us to keep climbing. Today's march will end at Peters Hut, now called Horombo Hut. A distance of 15 kilometres has to be covered and a difference in the height of 1,000 metres. That sounds harmless but, due to the thin air, a lot of people already suffer from headaches and breathing problems. We also have been told that heavy rain and snowfalls are common at this altitude. The muddy track and a heavy load on the shoulders can be a real hassle. Breakfast is a can of tomato juice, as we are in a hurry. As Max and I have worked in Addis Ababa, which lies at an altitude of 2,500 metres, we are used to some thin air. That, at least, is a small advantage.

The narrow track is soggy and overgrown with slippery tree roots. Despite my mountain boots, it takes a lot of concentration not to slip and fall with the heavy rucksack. Above us, the tops of the trees form a dense roof with the moss hanging down like women's hair. Lianas and bushes full of flowers make the forest seem impenetrable. Hidden birds begin their morning concert and, sometimes, rays of

Kibo on the left, Mawenzi on the right, altitude about 4.500 m

the rising sunshine on ferns and flowers which are covered with dew. The aromatic smells are a pleasure to inhale.

We swap our luggage every half hour as legs and lungs don't last any longer than that. Suddenly the forest opens up, and ahead of us is a flat mountain meadow. This is the limit of tree growth that is almost twice as high as in Europe. As far as the eye can see, there is an ocean of yellow flowers. Far away, the snow and ice-covered top of Kibo appears. Further, on the right, the black rocks of Mawenzi pierce the clouds. We move forward very slowly, giving our lungs a chance to adjust to the thin air. All the same, we still have to breathe deep and frequently. The beauty of the landscape is an unforgettable bonus for our efforts.

Lots of hills have to be climbed. Sometimes, small creeks rush down the narrow valleys. Or, the water simply runs along the path and makes us wade up to our ankles in mud. My mountain boots help a lot. Unfortunately, Max is wearing new boots of soft leather and gets wet feet immediately. Slowly, but faster than we can walk, dark rain clouds creep up the slopes. When they catch up with us, there still is no rain. But we put on our cardigans against the cold.

Every now and then, we meet people who are returning from the mountain. They all look tired and exhausted. When they see us carrying our own luggage, they sometimes look at us with admiration, but more often with expressions of pity. Other faces seem unable to show any feeling. Some climbers admit that they gave up long before they reached the summit. Well, we know by now that this mountain is not harmless. We have heard the story of how, recently, an Austrian had a heart attack up there and died. Also, apparently, a young man started spitting blood. But, both Max and I think that the best adventures are the ones that one survives. So, we keep climbing.

At midday, we have a good rest before we use the last of our energy to climb over the hill. Suddenly the Horombo Hut—a simple hut made of corrugated sheets is only a short distance away. We are at an altitude of 4,000 metres now.

Exhausted and with rattling lungs we proudly fall onto the wooden bunks. Now I feel the pressure on my temples. Max takes some tablets to ward off a headache. Dinner is just some bread and a can of white beans. For a few coins, porters of an American tourist group boil some tea for us.

Sunset from Kilimanjaro slope

Horombo Hut

After sunset the next day, the wind blows through the holes in the walls. It reminds me of a German January night! I creep into the sleeping bag with all my clothes on yet, I am still shivering. Due to the cold, sleep is hard to come by. Max has the same problems. Actually, he is worse off. He has not taken any malaria tablets and did not manage to kill all the mosquitoes in the Sikh temple. We think he might have contracted malaria. If so, we should cancel our climb. But Max thinks the cold will cool down his feverish state and wants to go on. It is a very risky decision. I have my own problem. The second finger of my left hand that I smashed on the train door in Ethiopia is still infected and hurts. But I am like Max. We don't give up.

In Horombo Hut, we slept on plain boards with no mattresses. In the morning cold, it takes a while for our stiff limbs to start working properly again. It is a taste of things to come. We hope to spend the next night in Kibo Hut but, we have another 1,000 metres to climb before then. We estimate that is another fifteen kilometres (ten miles). Kibo Hut is at the bottom of the slope of lava sand which leads to the summit. We sit down and make an inventory before we start walking. *How much longer can our bodies last?* One thing is for certain. If we keep carrying the rucksack, we will not even reach Kibo Hut. We open another can of beans for breakfast, roll up our sleeping bags in the army poncho and hang the roll over our shoulder.

We also fill the water containers as we have been warned that there is no more water available from here on. All we carry are our food supplies: two cans of tomato juice, some bread, some cheese, and we also take the photo bag … that is all we will take along. *Heia Safari!* God willing, we will make it to the summit, even if we only have tomato juice in our veins instead of blood. Soon after eight o'clock we start. Without the heavy rucksack, we feel better, almost relaxed. But we have to breathe very fast and frequently to fill our lungs with sufficient oxygen. Our legs are sore, but somehow, they keep going, and we make good progress. A narrow and flat valley leads us towards Mawenzi. Then, we arrive at a creek and a sign: Last drinking water.

We walk another few kilometres that take us to the end of the valley. There, we climb over rocks and see our destination. On the right is Mawenzi. To the left stretches the Saddle that goes all the way to the bottom of Kibo. Kibo Hut, where we are headed, can be seen as a small white spot in the distance. The Saddle looks like an easy walk. It is covered with stones and rocks, a few flowers, and some grass; this is surprising at this altitude. We realise that we are already well above the height of Mt.Blanc in Europe. Max walks too fast, and I follow him. And, after a while, we suffer the consequences: headaches, dizziness, increasing pressure on the chest. Our legs seem to be made of rubber, and we want to collapse. Long breaks become an absolute necessity. From now on, we agree that we will carefully walk step by step as if the ground below is thin ice. Despite this, the last few kilometres are pure torture. We stop more often and shorten the distances between rests.

It takes all of our willpower to keep going. Then, just after two o'clock, we finally reach Kibo Hut. We have covered fifteen kilometres

Kenya

Groggy! The white dot on the right is Kibo hut at 4.730 m

in six hours! Normally, that distance would have taken us about 3.5 hours. We have reached an altitude of 5,000 m by now. We take aspirin tablets for our headaches and try to get some sleep. I cover the sleeping bag with a big plastic bag to stop my body warmth from escaping too fast. We are already experiencing minus 10 degrees C. Max tries to ignore his fever, and similarly, I ignore the pain in my finger. We are dead tired and manage to sleep a few hours.

14.01.68

A Dutch couple shares the hut with us. They plan to reach Uhuru Peak at sunrise with an African guide. In order to reduce our risk, we decide to follow them—free of charge.

At ten to two in the middle of the night, we commence the journey. Max, with his fever, looks miserable but, he insists he must come along. He wears a tracksuit and straw hat for the occasion; it is still minus 10 degrees Celsius. At first, I feel all right. I wear long

Photo 1: Max and the porters of a tourist group have a rest.

Photo 2: Celebrating with Whiskey

Photo 3: The highest and dirtiest loo in Africa. Mawenzi in the background

pants and two cardigans under the windbreaker. A scarf covers my head under the hood. A shawl covers my mouth and nose, and I have covered my hands in woollen socks. While we are climbing, I even feel a bit warm. The slope is steep, and the sand feels firm, and in the glowing moonshine, I can even see where to place my feet. Then, when the moon hides behind the rocks, I use the torchlight as a backup.

I notice that Max is shaking in the cold so, I give him my shawl, the scarf, and the woollen socks. Now, we both feel the cold. The guide, an African, sings a German Christmas song: *"Ihr Kinderlein kommet"*(Come All Ye Children). Who would not want to follow him? But, the track is getting worse now and steeper.

We climb two steps and glide back one step on soft sand and gravel. It reminds me of the sand dunes along the North Sea. But the sand dunes at the ocean are not 800 to 1,000 m high. Gasping and coughing, we reach Hans-Mayer-Cave, a small hole offering protection from the wind.

The Dutch climber has a special hobby: he keeps vomiting, a side effect of the thin air. Max, with his soft leather shoes, keeps slipping and stumbling that makes him throw his arms up in the air attempting to rebalance. Meanwhile, I am suffering in the cold. Breathing is hard, and I have a pain in the side of my chest. Short rest periods do not change anything. At least, we have empty stomachs that protect us from vomiting.

At the Hans-Mayer-Cave, Max wants to give up. He wants to wait for the sunrise and return to Kibo Hut. But he realises that it would be too dangerous to climb down in the dark. However, the bigger risk is to fall asleep. He could die in the cold at this altitude and would turn into a block of frozen flesh. There is no choice but to keep going.

I have one advantage. I am so tired that I almost fall asleep while I am climbing. I tell my legs to keep walking regardless. They move as

Photo Above & Right: We have made it to Gillman's Point
Photo Below: Mawenzi from Gillman's Point. Sunrise and Moon Set on one photo. The moon gets reflected in a small lake of meltwater.

if they do not belong to my body. I hardly feel my toes. All I can think of is Gillman's Point, just that far and no further. I ignore the crystal-clear stars in the black night sky, just keep focusing on the rocks ahead between the opening in the glazier. I don't

Plaque on summit

look at my watch. I must just keep going. How long are five minutes? How long is half an hour? I forget Max. I forget the guide. I am I. And I have to keep going! Max falls backward. I have to catch him without falling … Otherwise, we will both roll down the slope. Soon, Max only falls forwards. How does he manage to get back on his feet? Forward, only forward. Tomorrow, we can be proud. Tomorrow we can write postcards. Tomorrow is far away. *Where the hell is Gillman's Point? Why does one have to write postcards? Why does one have to climb mountains? Why does one have to be proud? Are we idiots?*

"Five minutes to Gillman's Point!" sounds the voice of the guide.

What a relief to hear that but, they seem to be the longest five minutes of my life. Finally, we reach a gap in the rocks and some protection from the wind; we see a short flagpole. I fall to my knees and can hardly stop the tears. Is it weakness or joy or both? The time is a quarter to six on Sunday morning. Many people come up here every day. They all are proud and want to write postcards.

And all agree: "I will never climb this mountain again." Yet, many of them come back one day.

When we look back, we realise that it took us four hours to climb Kibo. Experienced climbers do it in half the time. Most tourists need six hours so, no wonder we are exhausted.

The Dutch couple finds enough energy to climb the last few hundred metres up to Uhuru Peak. We are cheating if we don't follow. If only I didn't feel so cold! Maybe … maybe, I can make it. But it is

1.

2.

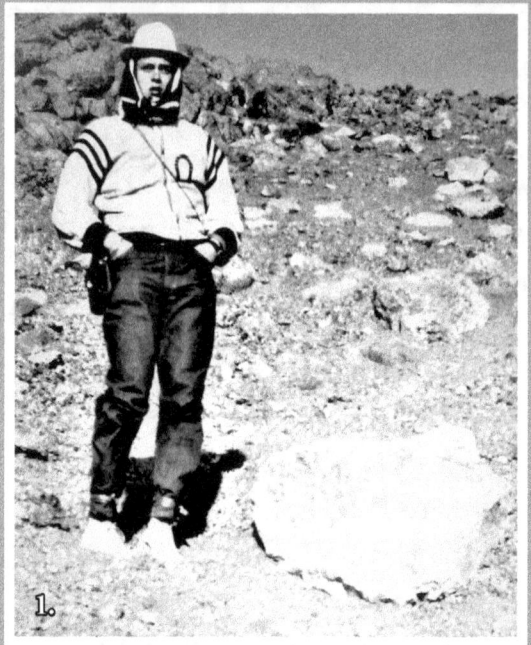

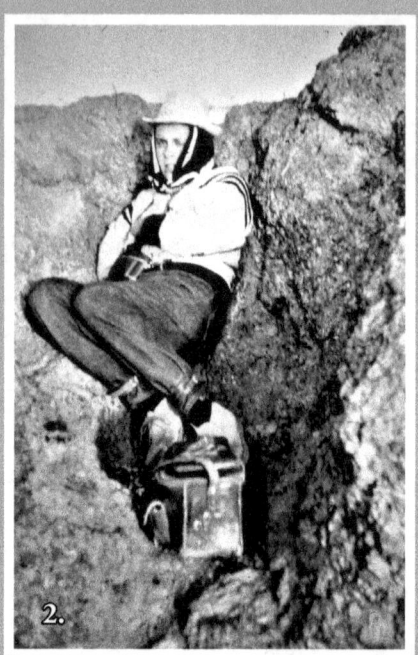

Photo 1: On the way down

Photo 2: Max has Malaria and 40 degrees fever.

Photo 3: Ratzel Glacier

Photo Below: Hans Meyer Notch

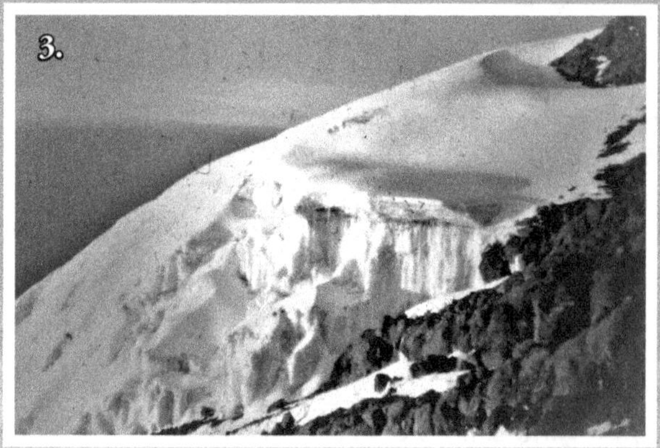
3.

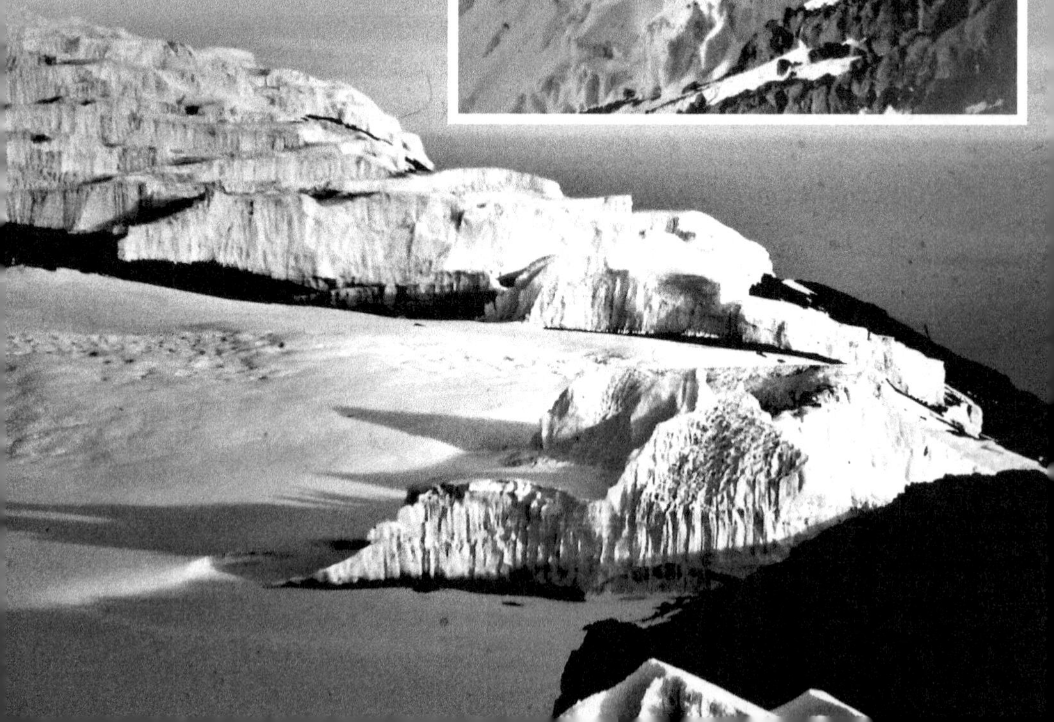

only a passing thought. Max cannot go any further, and I don't want to. We have reached the end of our strength. We have had it! We look for a gap in the rocks, huddle together for warmth, and wait for the sun. It takes almost an hour before it climbs up through a layer of clouds and fog.

My fingers are stiff from the cold when I take some photos. I have carried the camera under my clothes. The humidity caused by the warmth of the body freezes the shutter, and it breaks when I press the button. Luckily, I have a Retina-Camera as well, which I carried in my bag. The views are incredibly beautiful. But it is too cold to sit down and enjoy them for some time. We had hoped to walk to the crater in the middle of the mountain top but we realise that is too dangerous without a guide. One could fall into crevices in the glaciers. By 2021, these same glaciers have melted due to climatic change!

Soon we start the descent. It is almost fun. Sometimes, we simply glide down the sandy slope on our behinds.

We only make a short stopover at Kibo Hut and then, continue walking to Horombo Hut. Thankfully, my rucksack is still there. Max measures his fever; it is over 40 degrees C! He thinks that he must have malaria.

An African porter of an American group of tourists carries the rucksack back to Mandara Hut for me. He gets my windbreaker as a present. It does not often happen here that white people carry their own luggage and climb the mountain on their own. The Africans seem to admire us. One of them makes a couple of wreaths from a bunch of flowers and gives them to us to put around our hats. It means more to us than any Olympic Medal.

On the way back, I take my time and take photos of flowers. Max slowly follows other people. He urgently needs a bed and a doctor. I have almost reached Morombo Hut when I notice that my photo bag is not hanging on my shoulder anymore. I must have left it next to a flower about eight kilometres ago. Our vaccination cards, passports, and travellers' cheques are in that bag. Apparently, my brain stopped working properly at the altitude.

Despite the aching legs and the thin air, I march as fast as I can back the way I came to find the bag. That evening, I fall onto the wooden bunk bed, completely exhausted. The next morning, we make our way back to Moshi and relax on our beds in the Sikh Temple. I accompany Max to a doctor in a nearby hospital. He sticks a needle with "juice against Malaria" into the buttock of Max. It helps as, by the next day, the fever has disappeared.

The "Gold Medal"

CHAPTER 5:
Tanzania continued

Moshi
19.1.1968

We rest for a few days then, thank the Sikhs in the temple for their hospitality and make our way to the road to Dar es Salaam, the capital of Tanzania that is situated on the coast. The thumbs of our hands keep pointing to the east whenever a car passes us. We are hitchhiking again.

After a little while of walking on the road, the driver of a delivery van stops and gives us a lift for twenty miles to Lembeni. That is not much, but a start. When a public bus appears, we climb in and travel another eighty miles to Mombo. Then, after a short while, an Indian Sikh whom we know from Moshi stops and asks us to climb onto the back of his Peugeot van. We sit down on boards on both sides of a coffin—which we are told has a corpse in it—put our legs on the lid, and our bags on the floor. We mean no disrespect, and it is the only way we can make sure that the body does not get lost on the very rough road ahead. Our hands hold on to the roof rails. The Sikh fastens his turban and takes off at high speed like a fire

Sikh Temple in Moshi with Max and Peugeot van

engine. The road looks a bit like a corrugated sheet; it is not sealed. We leave clouds of dust behind us and breathe gritty air when other cars coming from the opposite direction pass us.

It is still night when we arrive at the Sikh Temple in Dar es Salaam after a 500 kilometres journey. There is a double bed under the stairs of the temple, which becomes our new home. We even get spoiled with some food and drinks.

The next morning, Max does not feel so well. His body plays up after suffering from malaria and the stress of climbing Mt. Kilimanjaro. He walks next to me without speaking a word; he is completely apathetic. I try to cheer him up and take him to a bar for a beer. Once there, at a table next to us, a young African lady with a blond wig invitingly spreads her legs under the table.

Trying to cheer him up, I ask Max, "Is that hair or flies?" He does not react. It makes me think that he must indeed be sick.

We visit the Swiss Consul and ask for help. He makes an appointment with an Austrian doctor who diagnoses a nervous breakdown and suggests that it may be best for Max to fly back to Switzerland. Max does not approve and, instead, he gets a prescription for a few different tablets. For about a week, the bed under the temple stairs becomes a hospital bed. After plenty of rest and proper food, Max reckons that he is fit again to "rip out trees".

Our next destination is Zambia. We will tramp along the "Hell Run", one of the worst "highways" in Africa.

Dar es Salaam
28.1.1968

Early in the morning, I pack my rucksack, and Max sticks all his belongings in his American soldier's bag. We say thank you and goodbye to the Sikh priest for his hospitality. Soon, we are walking along the road heading south and holding our thumbs up, trying to stop cars.

After barely a minute, a truck stops. The Indian driver takes us along to Morogoro, a distance of 190 kilometres, not bad for the start of our journey. Soon, we reach the other end of town. After half an hour in the hot African sun, we start swearing because no car comes along. Our hats at least stop us from getting a heat stroke.

Suddenly, a Mercedes 220SE races past us. It has a CD label on the back; this indicates that it is the car of a diplomat.

Australian Consul, his daughter, Max, driver

I say to Max, "Diplomats are not that special. He could have given us a lift."

A moment later, we hear the noise of a reverse gear. The Mercedes is returning. When we look inside the car, in the back seat is the Australian Consul for Tanzania. His daughter sits in the front seat and asks how far we plan to go.

I say, "Johannesburg."

She replies, "We are not driving that far. But is Iringa good enough?"

"No problem,' I say. I know that is a distance of 300 kilometres.

The African driver puts our bags in the boot. We let the Consul sit between us. He soon falls asleep and rests his head alternately on our shoulders.

After the heat, it is refreshing to sit in an air-conditioned car, racing along a dust road. But soon, the road becomes like a washboard. The driver has to slow down to protect the shock absorbers. When we meet oncoming cars, we end up in thick dust clouds hoping that there is no obstacle ahead. Even so, along the way, we have to stop once and exchange a flat tyre.

It is good luck that we are wearing the wreaths of flowers on our hats, the "Medal" for climbing M. Kilimanjaro. The Consul's daughter knows the meaning of this. She also thinks that I am an Australian soldier because of my German Boy Scout hat. It looks a bit like an Australian Army hat. Once we start chatting, it is apparent that is the reason why she asked her father to give us a lift.

The Consul invites us for a meal in a restaurant in a national park. In the evening, we arrive in Iringa, where the priest in the local Sikh temple welcomes us. The daughter of the Consul would love to stay there too but, for diplomatic reasons, her father cannot permit it. We take a shower, dress a bit smarter, and visit the restaurant in the best hotel in town. This time we have to pay for our meal, but we can

Photo Above: Max in the petrol truck
Photo Right: An accident, one of many

afford the luxury because we have spent no money today, and staying in the temple is free. Thank you to the Sikhs!

Early in the morning, Max and I stand on the road again. After one and a half hours, an Indian driver and his son stop their truck and take us along to Makumbako. On the way, we get spoiled again. The Indian calls us his guests and invites us for a big and tasty meal. We arrive in Makumbako in the evening and, after leaving us, the truck takes off in a different direction. This time, we spend the night on the floor of a bar. It is a small village, and there is no hotel or temple.

30.1.1968

Late in the morning, an African driver in a petrol truck with a hanger gives us a lift. It is Monday morning, and by now, we have covered 450 kilometres since we left Dar es Salaam. The driver is not supposed to take passengers along and, if discovered, he would have to pay a fine.

We assure him that we will pay the fine if that happens. We squeeze into the driver's cabin and mentally prepare for the "Hell Run". That is the nickname for the road ahead because of its bad condition and the many accidents.

During the rainy season, we have read the road is often closed and impossible to drive on. The rainy season is supposed to be finished but, today, the rain is pouring down like a waterfall. Sometimes, we travel for only ten kilometres in one hour. Frequently, the road looks like a river. In the deep stretches that we travel across, raging torrents cross the road and are up to fifty metres wide. Sometimes, they even carry uprooted trees.

In these situations, the drivers have to remain cold-blooded. The chance of crossing such rivers is 50:50. If the truck travels too slowly, it might get stuck, and the trucks have only one axle. If the driver puts his foot on the accelerator and goes too fast, the axle might break. Sometimes, the truck slips off the road and falls on its side due to the 40 tons of weight it carries.

At times, the driver stops, gets out of the truck, and walking slowly ahead with a stick he pokes around in the water to check if the narrow wooden bridge still exists underneath the flowing water. The drivers don't care if the truck falls on the side, as they are well insured. Hundreds of other drivers have had accidents before, sometimes caused by the many pot poles. Most of the trucks on the road are recent models, usually Fiat and *Officine Meccaniche* trucks from Italy. But soon, they look horrible. The cabin becomes full of cracks, and the shaking on the bad roads causes them to re-crack. If a hydraulic pipe breaks, it is hard to imagine how the driver can keep controlling the steering wheel.

Along the "Hell Run", which is 2,000 kilometres long, we count more than 100 trucks that have fallen on the side or are complete wrecks. Some of them have burnt and are only good for scrap metal. Sometimes, we come across a driver who is sitting on top of the cabin

"Hell Run"

and holding his bruised head is waiting for help. The governments, which operate the petrol transport industry, expect to write off 100% of all their trucks per year.

Next to Tanzania is Zambia, which is surrounded by land and has no oil industry and no pipeline. That is why petrol has to be imported by truck. The main export of Zambia is copper ingots. At this time, the Chinese are building a railway line parallel to the road but, that will take time to complete. It reflects a clever policy of China for development loans from western country banks often disappear into private bank accounts and other dark channels. The Chinese neither get paid back the loan nor the interest ... But the money is invested in useful projects, all the same, such as the railway line. The local governments soon become more dependent on China; they buy Chinese goods and yield to political influence. It is a milder form of Colonialism among superpowers competing for domination.

We are lucky not to have an accident and arrive late in the evening in Mbeya. We find a cheap hotel in town. An older African works there

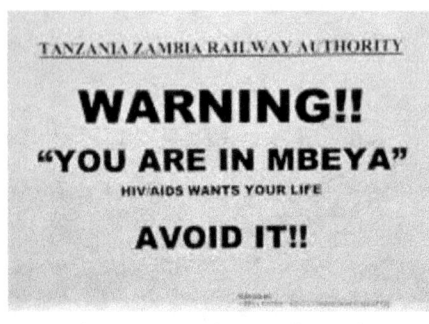
Street sign on the way to Lusaka

who speaks German. He tells us about his time as a cook at the court of Emperor William in Berlin, as Tanzania, at that time, was a German colony. The African organises some food with plenty of potatoes and even brings a young lady who gestures to join her in a separate room. But we have to say sorry, we are too tired for this kind of exercise after the long trip. We have also read the sign as shown in the photograph above. The Chinese railway workers must be frustrated because of the risks involved when touching some of the local girls.

In the morning, we are told that the road to the border with Zambia, formerly North-Rhodesia, is closed due to heavy rain. But we are lucky enough to find a Land Rover of the road patrol that takes us to the border post at Tondoma. On the way, a French mechanic joins us. He has to repair the cylinders of an engine in a Fiat tanker that got stuck in the mud on the side of the road.

There are no problems at the border and, soon after, we stop another truck, this time without a trailer. The two drivers, an Indian and an African, take turns driving at night. The Indian sleeps in the bunk behind the seats whilst his colleague drives throughout the night, trying successfully not to fall asleep.

But, for us, it is an awful trip. The road seems to have smallpox; there are potholes all over. They have to be navigated in first gear and very slowly. When other trucks pass us, they keep only a few centimetres from our truck in order not to end up in the mud beside the road. During this "Hell Drive", we can't fall asleep. We sit tightly squeezed together.

Once we disembark from the truck, a Rhodesian, in his Cortina, gives us another lift. Later that morning, we arrive at Kapiri-Mposhi where the road to Lusaka branches off. Lusaka is the capital city of Zambia. After half an hour, a Franciscan priest puts us in his truck and drops us at the home of a Reverend in Broken Hill. We can wash ourselves there and are given food and drinks.

Afterwards, the English reverend takes us to the edge of town, where we soon board another truck on the way to Lusaka.

We visit a small restaurant and order a couple of beers. Max pushes our bags in a corner and waits while I wander around looking without success for cheap accommodation.

Photo Right: Say "Cheese"
Photo Below: Luxury of the day: Tusker Beer

Frustrated, I enter a police station and ask if they have a cell where we can spend a night. The African police officer tells me we would have to break in somewhere or smash a shop window. That would cost more than a room in a hotel. The cheapest hotel room costs three pounds, and that exceeds our budget by far.

After two hours, I return to Max, and after a discussion, we decide to stay in the hotel. As we leave the restaurant, an English guy from Southern Rhodesia asks us where we have come from and where we want to go. We talk for a while. Then, he tells us to save the three pounds for the night and stay with him. We gladly accept his offer. Our host is a civil engineer and used to be a major in the British Army. In his home, he talks about his adventures during WWII at El Alamein and Tobruk, in North Africa, where he helped to force General Rommel and his German and Italian troops to retreat. A few beers help to strengthen the vocal cords, and we all have a good time. Bedtime finds us in our sleeping bags on the floor.

2.2.1968
The major has four bottles of beer for breakfast. We thank him for the hospitality and, at the side of the road, make the usual signs with the thumb of our right hand. A farmer arrives to give us a lift to Kafue at the border of Southern Rhodesia (now Zimbabwe). During the trip, he invites us for a meal in a restaurant. We feel lucky and cannot complain about our lives. But our mood soon changes when we walk across the Sir Otto-Beit-Bridge, which crosses the KafueRiver.

On a sign, we read that it is the second-longest bridge in Africa and one of the first hanging bridges in the world and was completed in 1939. In the middle of the bridge, is the border with Southern Rhodesia. Sadly, due to a lack of sufficient funds, we are not permitted to enter the country.

As the sun is setting, we know that it is not a good idea to spend the night in no man's land between the two white lines in the middle

of the bridge. Back on the Zambian side, the customs officer lets us sleep on the grass outside his office. He even organises for some food from an Indian restaurant, which is already closed, to be delivered.

As we eat our food, there are constant noises on the shortwave radio of the customs office. Sometimes one can hear some words. The customs officer is listening to the conversations of people known as Terrorists or Freedom Fighters who are hiding in the bush on the other side of the border. Only during the previous day, shots were fired at cars that entered Southern Rhodesia from Zambia. Rhodesia still has Ian Smith as a leader of a white minority that rules the country like a colony. It is internationally isolated and off-limits for businesspeople and tourists. Few countries maintain diplomatic relations. Well, we have to cross this obstacle.

The following day, we walk across the bridge again and ask the customs officer if we can ring our consulates in Salisbury, the capital city. The German consul lives in the office of the Swiss consul because his own consulate is closed. The German Government gives a guarantee for Germans who get stranded overseas or flies them back to Germany for taxpayer's money. They then confiscate the passport and hand it back only when the air ticket has been paid.

The German consul issues a guarantee for me. But I have to visit him in Salisbury and prove to him that I have had money sent to me from Germany.

My bank in Berlin has been instructed to send money from my account to me urgently anywhere in the world if requested. But, the Swiss are not that generous. Instead, the consul sends a telegram to the parents of Max and asks them to send some money. He gives a guarantee from his private funds until the money arrives. If none of this works, according to international law, Zambia would have to take us back. Maybe this might finally put us in jail.

After the backup is received from our consulates, we are permitted to enter the country. As quickly as we can, we walk away from the inhospitable customs office, covering five kilometres before a Portuguese gives us a lift to Salisbury. We realise that the terrorists may well have kept an eye on us through the zoom lenses on their rifles. Our mood improves after our driver shares three meals and some beer with us before we even reach Salisbury. The beer is like medicine for our upset nerves after such a bad start to the day.

After arriving in Salisbury, I send a cable to my bank and ask them to send a couple of thousand Deutsche Marks. Expecting to soon have some funds, we move into the Elizabeth Hotel. It will cost us 30 shillings per night and is inclusive of breakfast. Warm showers and clean bedsheets are a welcome change. However, thinking about it later, I realise that I have forgotten to look for a Sikh temple.

While we are waiting for our money to arrive, we explore the town, visit the National Gallery of Art, and watch a movie. The local beer is quite tasty too. After the money arrives, we visit the consuls and thank them for their assistance.

In Salisbury, one can see only the positive sides of Colonialism. The European inhabitants may only be a small minority, but one can notice the traces of their activity: there are modern and good-looking buildings, sealed roads, better-dressed African people, new cars, and good restaurants with reasonable prices. Unfortunately, all this happens on the backs of the majority of African people who work for low wages in their own country. Thanks to their skin colour and a lack of education, they are also looked down on as less intelligent.

According to the Dutch Reformed Church of the Boers in South Africa, the Old Testament recounts how Cain killed his brother, Abel. The Africans are supposed to be the descendants of Cain and, as a punishment, have to be the cheap helpers of the white descendants of Abel. This philosophy of Apartheid has its effect even in Rhodesia. Nevertheless, we are still headed to the country of the Boers, the "white tribe of Africa" which will be our next and final destination.

Romantic Africa (Postcard)

For the Head Office of the Communists in Moscow, the conditions in the last remaining colonies in Africa are a welcome reason to support revolutions with arms and propaganda. But apart from arms and ideology, the Russians have little to offer. Newly independent countries soon experience a decline in the administration and economy. In my opinion and from what I have read and seen, corruption and crimes increase. Competition and tribal wars due to different languages and cultures delay the development. Borders were drawn by colonial powers like England, France, and Germany, disregarding tribal territories and their borders. Once the white people leave the countries, then apart from the Russians, only the United Nations and the Chinese can offer alternative help. Africa appears to be reverting into darkness. When will a rainbow appear on the horizon?

On a Saturday morning, we stand at the road to the south again. It is in good condition with plenty of traffic heading to South Africa. As a goodbye gesture from Salisbury, it starts raining. We hide under the roof of a garage until the sun shines again. By now, it is four o'clock. Finally, a funny old farmer takes us along to Gatooma. Once we arrive there, we start searching for a hotel. Another farmer and his wife interrupt us and invite us to travel with them to Bulawayo. In Gwelo, we all stay in a hotel. Our hosts tell us that they are building a yacht in which they will soon start on a trip around the world. We wish them good luck!

The next morning, we have a big breakfast before we head out to Bulawayo. We thank the future world travellers for their assistance. They take us to the border of the town, and the next lift is only for two kilometres. Then, a farm lady with two kids invites us into her car. We move another twenty kilometres on the map.

In the Chevrolet-Impala of another farmer, we end up in Gwanda, where our first Boer picks us up with his Opel-Kapitän and takes us to West Nicholson. In between, he visits an Asbestos refinery. Max and I spend the night in the guest room of a garage.

10.2.1968
It is Saturday, and an African driving a Nissan van moves us forward another fifteen kilometres. We are very lucky when a young South

Beit Bridge, Car of Revel Ellis

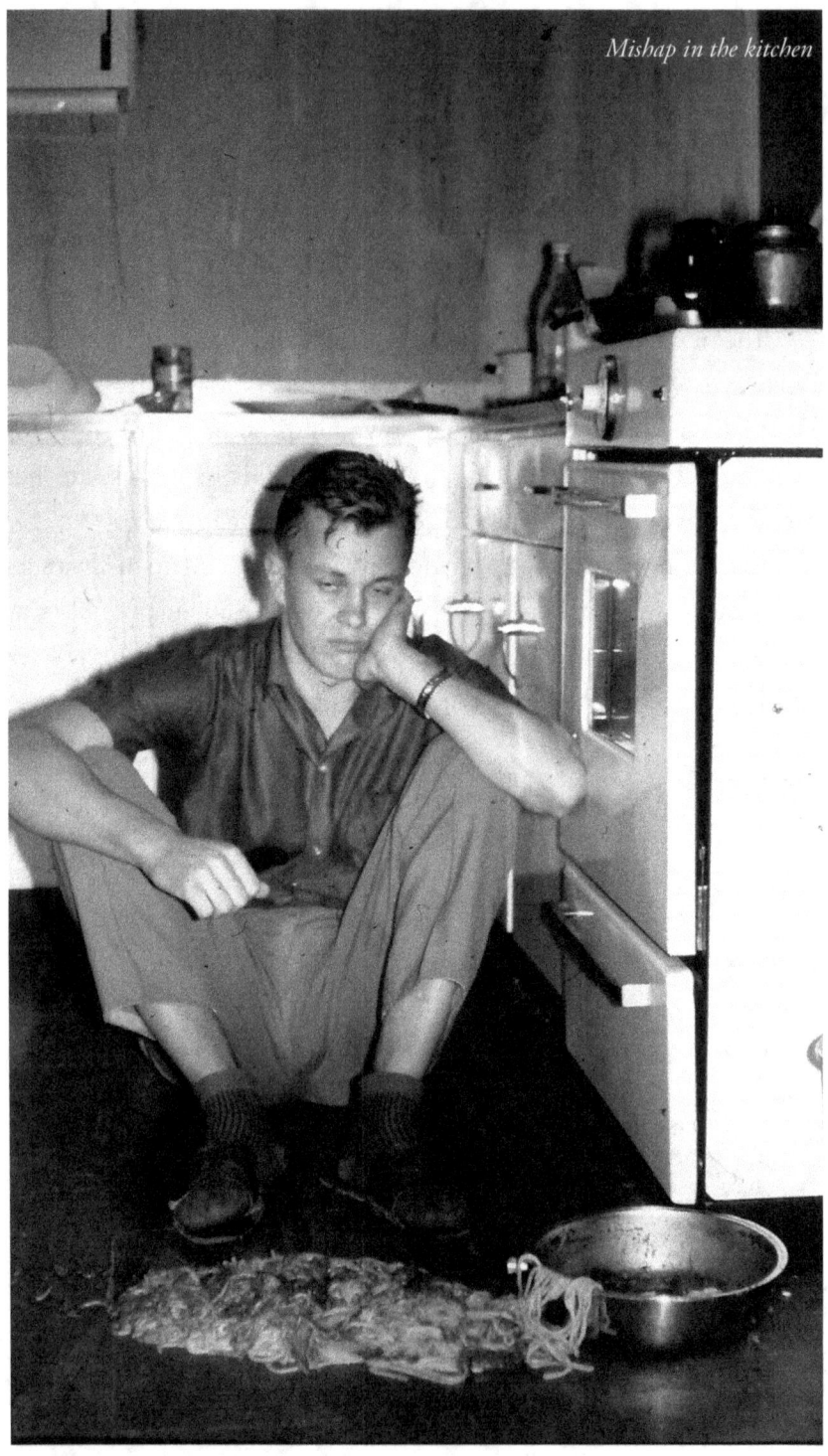

Mishap in the kitchen

African by the name of Revel Ellis offers to take us in his blue Volkswagen all the way to Johannesburg. We gladly accept the offer.

Soon, we reach the border on the other side of Beit Bridge. On the Immigration Form, the race has to be entered. I write Arian, making myself whiter than the Boers, my first contact with Apartheid.

The Immigration officer says, "Why don't you wait until you have seen the country?"

We pass the Verwoerd-Tunnel and Pretoria, the capital city and seat of Government, and late at night, we arrive at the home of the Ellis family in Johannesburg. We get invited to stay for the night, and after dinner, we are grateful to sleep in comfortable beds.

Mrs Ellis receives a big bunch of flowers from us during the next day to say thank you. Sadly, Mr Ellis lies in bed and has to use a breathing machine. During WWII, he became a prisoner of war and had to work in coal mines in Germany. The dust damaged his lungs. Now the end of his life is near but, he indicates to us that he is happy to have German tramps as guests.

We have travelled the distance from Dar es Salaam to Johannesburg in two weeks, a record of being proud of. My travels started on 4.10.1964, in Berlin. I arrived in Jo'burg on 10.2.1968. Three years and four months have passed. The ultimate destination is Cape Town where I plan to spit in the sea. But that will have to wait. I have to save some money first.

After a couple of days, we meet Reiner Gottschalk from Berlin, who came to South Africa on his bicycle; another interesting story. We rent a flat

Our new home: "Splendid Place"

on the eighteenth floor of a building near the city and start looking for work.

CHAPTER 6:
South Africa

Johannesburg
01.02.1968

How long will Max and Reiner, and I stay in South Africa? Answer: At least until we have saved enough money to continue our travels. On arrival, we automatically receive a Temporary Residence visa. We can legally look for work. The percentage of white or European inhabitants in South Africa is less than 20%. For that reason, we could easily apply for citizenship to help increase the numbers of the white population. If only this country would not be ruled by the policy of Apartheid! As far as I am concerned, it is a form of modern slavery.

Within a week, we are working. I end up with Siemens, a large German telephone and electronics manufacturing company. There is plenty of paid overtime, and my savings account balance increases quickly.

South Africa is a very beautiful country with its endless beaches, mountain ranges, and savannas. There is the famous Kruger National Park with its animal herds and the *"Bantustans"* (Homelands) with

View of Hillbrow from our balcony

a variety of at least eighteen African tribes or nations with different languages and cultures. The most well-known of these are the Zulus. The Africans in their "Homelands" are, in my opinion, kept like animals in their nature reserves. It is not permitted to go there without special permission otherwise, one ends up in jail.

Further, it is illegal to mix with Africans unless one is a boss and gives them work to do. Having African girlfriends is almost as criminal as using drugs. The system gets enforced by Terrorism and Immorality laws. For a newcomer, it is hard to stay out of trouble, especially Germans, who are known for their love of black 'bread'.

Some of my experiences are worth mentioning: Near our house is Joubert Park. The park benches have been painted brown and have labels stating EUROPEANS ONLY. I see a white baby lying on a bench with its African nanny sitting on the grass.

My company is situated in a high-rise building. The lifts in the foyer have the same blue label as in the park. A lift on the side has a brown label stating *NIE BLANKES* (Non-whites). When no one is watching, I take a few labels off with my screwdriver and keep them as souvenirs. If I would be seen, there might be a reason to arrest me under the Terrorism Act.

Banks and post offices have separate entries. In the double-decker buses, the last bench on the ground floor is reserved for Africans. The top floor is mixed. Railway stations have separate platforms; the bus stations too.

One night, I see some Africans at the bus station dancing in a circle. They let me squat in the middle with my tape recorder and dance around me, holding their sticks *(Knobkerries)* with one hand up in the air. Suddenly, a police car stops close by. An officer calls me to come to him and asks me where I am from.

I reply, "Jo'burg."

He must notice that I am a foreigner and says, "Don't let me see you here again."

I throw a packet of cigarettes into the circle of dancers, wave at them, and disappear. They laugh and keep dancing.

One day, I have to visit the German consulate in a high-rise building in the city. A Boer (White South African with Dutch ancestry) sits on a chair and drives the lift when a "Coloured" (mixed-race)

Pretoria:
BLANKES
ALLEEN
(Whites only)

Such signs can be seen all over South Africa

man with a toolbox gets in. The lift does not move. The Boer tells the man to get out of the lift. The man replies that he is a mechanic and has to repair the lift motor, which is hard to reach from the staircase.

I put my arm around his shoulder and say, "I will climb the stairs with you and carry your toolbox." As we walk to the stairs the lift starts moving without us.

In the town of Upington, near the border with Namibia, I walk around at sunset. Suddenly, a siren starts blaring like in Berlin before the bombs fell during WWII. A young African girl approaches me and asks if she can walk with me like a servant. She tells me that Africans have to leave the town before sunset, or they can get arrested. I walk with her up to the surrounding landscape.

In Windhoek, the capital of Namibia, I stay in "Berg Hotel", a name left over from the German colonial days like "Goering Street" from the Nazi area, and a restaurant called "Thüringer Hof." At weekends, a band entertains the guests. When that happens, I go down the stairs into the cellar with another two whites and dance with the African female servants while the band plays on the floor above us.

At work in Jo'burg, an African girl pushes a trolley around and distributes coffee and tea. She asks me, "Do you want to have your coffee black or white?"

I reply, "I like it coloured."

She giggles and pours very little milk into my cup. A female Boer colleague nearby tries to kill me with her eyes.

In a pub, an African servant cleans the floor. A customer puts a 50-cent coin on a bar chair. When the African wants to pick it up, the coin gets pushed onto the floor. He picks it up before I can do it for him. They call that "Small Apartheid". People like me are called "Kaffir Booties", friends of the Africans.

For some time, I work as an accountant on a construction site at Eros Airport near Windhoek. A worker has an accident and is badly hurt. When the ambulance arrives, the driver refuses to take the injured man because he is African. The hospital is for Whites Only. He leaves quickly before the white employees can beat him up. They put the patient on a wooden board on a truck and take him to an aeroplane which the company has hired. It takes him to a distant African hospital. The company is an American one. Would that happen in a local company?

On my way home after work, an African on the road nearby gets hit by a car. Bypassers drag him to a wall against which he can sit. A white doctor examines him. I stop a car with an African driver

Barotse dance

Bush toilet

Valley of 1.000 Hills, one of the "Homelands" in South Africa

and ask him to please take the injured man to an African hospital in another suburb. He agrees. As I keep walking, I hear a voice behind me, "He helped our brother." Is what I have done very unusual?

At work one day, I ask an old African with white hair which makes photocopies in a small office, "What do you think of Boers?"

His answer: "They kill our hearts every day."

In Durban, I am hungry and see an Indian restaurant that sells Curry Rice and Chicken. As I walk in, I notice that it is for NON-WHITES. I ask the waiter if I may come in. He tells me to sit behind the stairs where I am hidden from the view of police walking past. This adds a special flavour to my meal.

Germans like black bread. Some of them spend the nights with their African girlfriends on rooftops behind the lifts, in factory bathrooms, or among bushes in parks. Some get caught, and end up in jail and then get kicked out of the country. Immorality can get fined with a sentence of up to seven years in jail. That applies mainly to locals. Some "sinners" go for a walk with their African girlfriend, with her always walking five metres behind them. They stop, every now and then, and look at separate shop windows.

At one stage, Max has to move away to work in another city so; we give up our flat. Reiner and I move into a small flat near Central Station. People call the area the "Murder Mile". One evening, as I cross a side street, I see a white fellow lying face-down in the middle of the street. I bend down to see what is wrong when he suddenly points a pistol at me. He wants my wallet. I quickly step aside and keep walking. Now I understand why it is called the Murder Mile.

I could go on with similar stories. But who wants to know? It is all history now, in 2021.

Whilst living in South Africa, once a month, Max and I join a few other friends and travel some 400 kilometres by car to Swaziland for an "oil change." Swaziland is a small landlocked independent African Kingdom between South Africa and Mozambique. Apartheid is not known there.

In Germany, they say the cherries taste best in the neighbour's garden, especially when it is forbidden to pick them, hence, our trips to Swaziland and the freedom it affords us. All the same, the police once knock on the door of our hotel room and ask for our passports. They

"Murder Mile" in Johannesburg with our balcony on the right

seem to inform the police in South Africa. Once, when I was working in Namibia, a police officer visited Max and Reiner in Johannesburg and asked what we were doing in Swaziland. My friends tell him that we are visiting with friends. No further questions get asked.

At long weekends, there was sometimes enough time to drive all the way to Laurenco Marques (now known as Maputo) in Mozambique, which is still a Portuguese colony. There too, life is normal and (without Apartheid). Africans can even vote if they have attended school long enough. It is what we regard as Africa with a relaxed South European flavour. When visiting, we once even watch Portuguese-style bull fights there.

In Swaziland, one of the main attractions is a water well near Mbabane where hot water bubbles up from a large pipe in the ground. A swimming pool has been built around it. When we arrive there with our African girlfriends, South African people in the pool disappear, and we have the pool to ourselves. It is winter, nighttime would see us dancing around the pool naked to African music from

A "Guest House" in Swaziland. Goodbye dance in the morning.

Photo Above: Swazi pool in the daytime. Reiner, Max, Johannes

Photo Below: King Sobhuza II at a Reed Dance

Photo Right: Asking for the way – in vain

the tape recorder. Then, we jump into the hot water, enjoying the music and sharing a cool beer with our girlfriends. Decency does not permit me to print the photos.

Once a year, the Reed Dance Festival takes place and lasts for eight days. At this time, thousands of girls and unmarried women from the various chiefdoms from all over the country converge on a large open area where guests sit on a tribune. The girls and women have to be virgins.

This status gets checked before they can take part in the feast, as this event is a celebration of their chastity. On arrival, the girls carry bush knives and bundles of reeds which they have cut as a symbol of virginity.

The reeds get donated to the Queen Mother for repairs of the fence of the royal compound, which is a mixture of modern buildings, including the parliament and some traditional houses.

Much of the dancing by these virginal women gets done topless. At the end of the feast, the king chooses one of the women as his future wife. Thus, he ends up with a large harem. King Sobhuza II, who invented the festival in the 1940s, is supposed to have at least seventy wives. It may be a way to have friendly relations with the chiefs of the Kingdom. I meet one of his wives in a restaurant, and she spends the night with me. She wears a red cord around her hips, which is the only item she does not take off. I think to myself, *Is it an African Chastity belt?*

30.4.1970

Finally, it is time to say goodbye to Africa. After more than two years, our bank accounts look healthy again but, a country full of hate is not where I want to spend the rest of my life.

Max and I plan to visit the World Exhibition in Osaka in Japan and pay a short visit to all the countries on the way there. There is plenty of water between Africa and the Asian continent.

Also, the winds of change are blowing from the horizon. Apartheid will come to an end a few months after Max and I depart South Africa. Luckily, it happens without a civil war. Reiner, however, decides to stay for a few more years.

CHAPTER 7:
Leaving South Africa

Madagascar, Mon Amour

First, we hop across to Madagascar. It is our first evening in Tananarive (now known as Antananarivo) and our first walk around the capital city of Madagascar. The road is dark, with only a few lamps spreading their light. Around us is the noise of traffic. We smell the smoke of wood fires, the manure of chicken and straw. The air between the houses is warm and humid.

Max shouts, "Shit," and disappears from my side.

I look around, startled to see him climbing up from a large hole in the footpath. Brown people walk past laughing about Max.

The present seems to be unreal. Our minds are still in Johannesburg ... it is a thousand miles behind us in the southwest, in the middle of South Africa. In the age of jet planes, distances shrink. New impressions seem to follow each other in split seconds.

This morning we drank our last beer at Jan Smuts Airport in Jo'burg. We got pressed against the backrests of our seats when the plane of Air Madagascar rose into the sky.

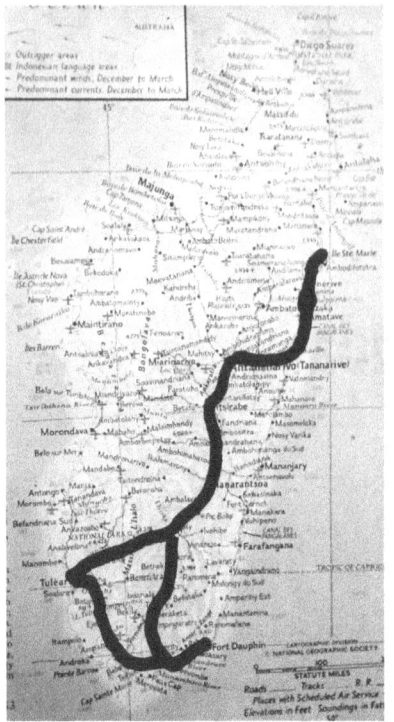

Photo Above: My first trip to Madagascar.
Photo Below: Max in the Zoo in Tananarivo

We listened to the voice of the stewardess as she announced, "Ladies and gentlemen, we welcome you on our flight from Johannesburg to Tananarive."

This was said in French, and that is when we realised that our English would not be of much use in Madagascar. However, as I learned a bit of French when I worked in Egypt, it should come in handy on the big red aisle.

Max and I have a last glimpse at the hills of sand tailings from the gold mines around Johannesburg, and then, the plane crosses the East-Transvaal and Swaziland. I think of Esther Dhlamini, Esther Shongwe, and others, that will never see me again. African music and dancing, parties in the hot pool, and curly hair under nylon wigs will never be forgotten. And, we are happy to depart South Africa, a country that is supposed to mainly be enjoyed by people with no brown pigment in their skin. We will try to erase that country from our memory.

After a short stop for refuelling in Laurenco Marques, we cross the channel of Mozambique. I wonder, *Does the daughter of a Zulu chief in a slum of LM still think of me?*

Clouds race past against the dark blue sky. Soon, the yellow sand of a beach and the white frills of breaking waves appear, followed by bushland and the curves of dried-out riverbeds. The huts and houses of the small town of Marondave in Madagascar greet us. Next, we fly over the Central Highland with green plants and fertile soil and enough water for agriculture to thrive. After four hours, the wheels of the plane hit the runway of Antananarivo. The short names of Tananarivo and Tana get used mostly by the local people.

The good-looking police lady who puts the stamp in the passport says *"Salama tubko"* (Good day) in Malagasy. It is a Polynesian language that has been put into writing by Catholic missionaries. I have read that, long ago, the ancestors of the inhabitants migrated here in their outrigger boats from the area of Eastern Indonesia. Many people speak French as well, a useful souvenir of the long French colonial administration.

In a room of "Hotel Smokey Joe" situated at the railway station, a big French bed waits for me. It is not my first trip to Madagascar, and Juliette has waited for me for one year. Last time, I tramped on a truck down to the tip of the island at Fort Dauphin and had a

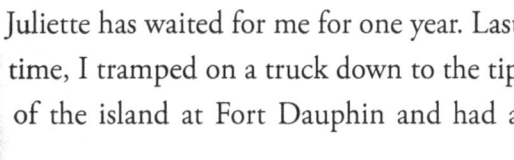

Photo Above: President Philip
Photo Right: Tsiranana Antanarivo (Antananarivo)

Colette and Max

look at the pirate island refuge of Isle St. Marie further up on the east coast. It is now a paradise for tourists who like to swim.

Tananarive
1.5.1970

Today is a celebration, the day of the workers. In the morning, people assemble early on the square in front of the station. They wave flags, wear costumes, and carry placards with political slogans. Music fills the air with guitars, drums, flutes, and accordions. In between, violins can also be seen. Sometimes, the music sounds Polynesian or like French country dances.

The Rue de Independence is very crowded. It is a wide road with arcades on both sides. The vendors squat on mats and offer their goods. It is the most colourful market I have seen. There is bargaining and plenty of laughing while groups of workers and pupils are marching past. There is a general relaxed feeling in the air of people who are not in a rush like in central Europe. Men wear straw hats. Women wear hats too and *"Lambas"* around the shoulders that are made of soft cotton material. Mothers suckle their babies in public. A woman at a market table collects lice from the curly hair of another lady. I watch

Juliette, sister of C., and Manfred

on as a fellow stands up on a wooden crate, makes a speech, and supports his points by swinging his arms in the air. If he is lucky, later on, someone may buy him a bottle of beer. I cannot take my eyes off the girls with their soft copper brown skin, the oval eyes of Malays, their slim bodies, and their elegant way of walking.

In the highland of Madagascar, the Hova people are the majority of residents. They have a lighter skin colour and run the government. There are another twenty tribes distributed over this huge island. A hundred years ago, the Hova, with the help of French advisors, conquered most of Madagascar. Their most powerful enemies were the Sakalava, Baro, and Antandroy tribes. Full independence from France was achieved in 1960, and it is hoped that the Hova people will voluntarily share their rule with others.

As I look around the celebrations, I see that there is no arguing and no fighting. The police and soldiers stand at strategic points in their uniforms and hold machine guns ... But the guns have no magazines. Maybe the 1st of May is only a formality because the few rich people in this country are

Drummer of a military band

A little night music in a "restaurant"

not interested in socialism, and the uneducated people don't know what that means.

In the evening, some alcoholic makes rude comments about the president. A woman smacks the drunk's face. The girls that are accompanying us get excited, climb onto the window sill, spit down to the street and pour out the ashtrays. I sit back amused, wondering, *Why don't they throw the empty beer bottles as well?* A young man with a white shirt and necktie pulls the drunkard away from the angry people around him.

After a long sleep, the next morning, we take a taxi to Besarety, where our girls live. What a surprise! There are no tin shacks or wooden walls with a tin roof. We don't see any homeless dogs searching for food scraps in heaps of rubbish or beggars in rags. The houses are made of mud bricks and have pointed roofs with slates. Many window frames and doors have been painted recently. We are in a rural but clean environment. On the side of the roads are water pumps, maybe each for a block of houses.

All the same, the rooms are small with just enough space for a bed, a narrow table, a sofa, and a chair. Clothes hang on a nail on the door. Colourful pages from a calendar decorate the walls. Empty cigarette packs have been stuck in between them and the names on the packs give away the countries from which former boyfriends came … cigarettes that cannot be bought in Madagascar. Due to the lack of space, the four of us spend the afternoon sleeping on the bed.

After sunset, we explore the nightlife. Today is a Kermises—a Malagasy Oktoberfest— organised by the government every year on this day. In some rooms, one can throw dice or play roulette or join the young people dancing in different halls. The bands use electric guitars, drums, and accordions. European song hits are followed by the fast beat and beautiful sound of the local songs. Different bands seem to have a volume competition and the dance floors are crowded; shoulder hits the shoulder. In the semi-dark rooms, white eyes in brown faces show the enjoyment after some glasses of beer. No one gets upset when they step on other dancers' feet; many dance barefoot anyway. The entertainment is set to last all night but, Max and I soon get tired and hop into our hotel beds after midnight.

We spend most of the next day in bed too, as we suffer from dysentery. This appears to be a *malaise* that is the entrance fee into Third World countries. We keep vomiting and take Mexaform tablets. Juliette comes to visit and stays with me; she makes me feel better.

Tananarive spreads over seven hills like Rome in Italy. My legs complain when I have to walk to the German Embassy in the city. On the highest hill is the Royal Castle. It has an adventurous history. The queens and kings who ruled from there had very long names, and they are hard to pronounce. One king was called Andrianamporinimerina! He permitted the English and French Missionaries to spread the Christian religion across the Kingdom. This new religion spread faster than smallpox.

At the same time, European tradesmen and scientific ways of thinking were introduced. One missionary translated the whole Bible and read it to the king. He was very impressed and called a recently trained carpenter to build a few wooden crosses for the next capital punishments. He had not heard of this method and was intrigued.

In the days of Napoleon, France and England were fighting for control over the Indian Ocean. Even at the court in Madagascar, they manoeuvred against each other. Religion typically became a tool in big power politics And, when Queen Ranavalona was in power, she decided to forbid Christianity. All Europeans had to leave the country. A local woman by the name of Rasa Lama became the first martyr. The story goes that on the edge of a cliff, she was asked by officials to revoke the religion. In silent answer, she knelt and prayed. The spears of the palace guards killed her, and they threw her body over a cliff near her palace … The rats at the bottom of the cliff had plenty to eat that night.

All Bibles that could be found were burned; churches and Christian schools were destroyed. Christians who did not get killed went into hiding, surviving in caves and other safe places whilst waiting for better times. Apparently, during this time, one of them learned the whole New Testament by heart.

I have often wondered whether it is a result of the persecution that today, almost all of the Malagasy people are Catholic Christians. *It would be ironic, wouldn't it?* Their traditional gods still exist in the background, like small gods under the one big God, Father, Son, and the Holy Spirit. In effect, this is a multiplication of the Trinity. Perhaps, the strict adherence to traditional beliefs was a reason why the new missionaries quietly tolerated the other gods?

After a week, in Tananarivo, we squeeze our bags and ourselves into a taxi and take off to the bus station at the edge of town. We leave a couple of sad young ladies behind. What they do is not prostitution, but a way to try to get married to a foreigner and escape for a better life in a rich country. For that reason, I always treat them like ladies.

In Madagascar, it is an honour to have a child from a European. It earns respect. The tolerance of the Malagasy makes it possible that people of mixed race are fully accepted. They are not "Coloureds" like in South Africa. They are only called *"Café au Lait"* (Coffee with Milk). I cannot think of a more charming description.

At the bus station, our bags get tied to the roof rack of a *"Taxi-Brousse"*. We take off on a road that winds around many bends but is still sealed. Our destination is the Itasy-Lake and Ampefy, a small village on the western bank of the lake. Upon arrival, we find a small cottage that belongs to a large hotel nearby. Around us, it looks like the Black Forest in Germany. The tops of extinct volcanoes reach for the sky. At a distance of about 200 metres, a waterfall rushes over black lava rocks. At the beach, mineral water oozes from the sand. We are advised not to swim in the lake because of the crocodiles. *Oh sorry!*

Max films a crocodile "Man-eater."

We do not not want to disturb the man-eaters, but Max at least wants to film them.

Due to the fresh and clean air around us, we sleep like gods. Ampefy, the town, is also sleepy, and one must walk slowly. The only road is a few hundred metres long and has no streetlights. Sleeping dogs open their eyes when the torchlight shines on them. The only pedestrians are ducks with flat feet gliding over the asphalt like British Guard soldiers at Buckingham Palace.

The light of a kerosene lamp shines onto chicken droppings through the open door of the Hotel Soa. Inside, a few men sit at a shaky table, eat rice and fish, and drink coffee. With their shoulder cloth and straw hats, they look like Mexicans. The young daughter of the hotel owner walks around barefoot and carries a baby in a blanket over her back. She serves the guests. In a corner, kids hide and giggle, but they come to us when we offer them biscuits. The voices of birds can be heard under the black and star-studded sky. From a radio emanates the soft and melodious singing of Malagasy ladies singing the latest hit parade.

Max, Werner and my rucksack

Ampefy
10.5.1970

The Lili Waterfalls are about ten kilometres from Ampefy. Max prefers to stay behind and have a rest. I walk on over winding hilly tracks and through valleys. I become lost because the farmers don't understand my few words of French, and I think, the waterfall may also have a different name in their language. I finally find the Lili Falls but, I must have walked for twenty kilometres. My water bottle is empty, and my legs are sore. But, when I look around the landscape and the waterfall, they are a feast for my eyes.

A fisherman cooks coffee for me over his charcoal fire. Then, I notice a Malagasy who is repairing is German DKW Moped, which was built in 1967. I pay him a tip, and he allows me to ride with him back to Ampefy. It is a very rough track, and I am surprised that the little machine can climb up steep hills with the weight of two men. I become even more respectful of the "Made in Germany" mark printed below the backlight. Malagasy natives who see us pass by start to laugh and cannot seem to stop. I must indeed look funny with the neck protection of my cap of the French Foreign Legion.

The next morning, Max and I climb into a minibus planning to reach Antsirabe that is located about 150 kilometres further south. The bus only goes as far as Soavinandriana, and this journey takes an hour.

Then, after a few hours, another *Taxi-Brousse* takes us to Faratsiho. We are thrown around on our seats like on horses in a rodeo. The rainy season has just ended and, since the road is not sealed, there are deep scars on it. Our taxi also has to climb over some of the highest mountain passes in Madagascar. Steep descents around many bends and across shaky wooden bridges sometimes make one forget to look at the beautiful landscapes. I cannot hold on to a rail because I press the tape recorder and the camera against my body with both hands. Sitting on top of the back wheel makes the up and down motion

Visiting a local family in Antsirabe

much worse, and watching me provides entertainment for the other passengers. It is evening, by the time we reach Faratsiho, where we are to stay for the night.

We find seats for our sore 'behinds' in a small restaurant. Our dinner is rice with a lot of meat, some eggs, and a few beers. Nearby is a small hotel with a room for us. The walls are made of hardened mud with a roof of straw. Next to the bed is a shaky table with a candle. Our bed is a wooden frame on which boards have been nailed with a mat on top. The bed is also not level. Max and I crawl into our sleeping bags and lie close together because of the cold and the risk of rolling onto the floor of hardened soil. Max makes use of his can of insect spray to avoid flea bites. We feel like American movie stars falling asleep in a cloud of perfume. For the couple of dollars that we have spent, it would be foolish of us to expect more. Oh! I forgot to mention that Werner, is a friend of Max's, and he has joined with us for part of the way. He has to sleep next to our bed on the floor. Soon, he will return to South Africa.

Breakfast consists of a sip of cold water from my bottle. We have to hurry up as the bus to Antsirabe is scheduled to leave at 6 am and it is already full to the rooftop with passengers. Max manages to sit next to the driver. Werner and I have to climb in through a window via the ladder in the back of the bus. I end up in a corner. A Malagasy pours some black pepper from a small flask into my hand. It makes the dust taste better as the back wheels of the bus throw it into my face once we get going. Another passenger gives me a plastic bag to protect my tape recorder. The camera is in hiding already under my shirt and windbreaker. Our "rodeo-drive" through the road's potholes takes three hours before we reach Antsirabe. I get down from the bus, covered in dust.

As we make our way to the Petit Casino, we realise that it may be the most sleazy hotel in town. But, it is all that we can afford and, in our room, there is a clean toilet and a functioning cold shower. At night, the young people meet here, play soccer on machines, and drink beer. Music from the music box and girls make the French beds vibrate. It is a swinging hotel!

The next day, a local family invite us over to their house. I manage to record some Malagasy music from their record player. But, more interesting to us men are the three daughters. They don't speak English. Yet, we still can have a dance party in the living room. When the mother does not watch, we pull them close to us. They are of mixed blood and have beautiful hair. I have a gut feeling that I would soon be married if I were to stay in Antsirabe much longer; my friends agree with me when we chat about this later.

Back at our hotel, I meet Josephine Ezeni from Fort Dauphin. She belongs to the tribe of the Antanosi. Unfortunately, she does not speak English either but, she has no mother to watch over her. I spend most of the next day 'sleeping'. The next night, we have another dance party with the long-haired girls.

Antsirabe
16.5.1970

We get up early. Antsirabe is too expensive as we are drinking too much beer. Also, spending too much time in one place is no good for our travel budget. It is still a long way to our final destination: the World Exhibition in Japan.

Before the bus takes off, however, there is time to visit the cattle market. The people of Madagascar don't have much money, and their wealth is measured by the number of cattle they own. Due to the ever-increasing need for pastures, most of the forests on the highland have already been chopped down; this is an environmental disaster.

At lunchtime, we climb into a *Taxi-Brousse*. The road to Betafo is sealed and will be the last sealed road for a long time. At Betafo, a road to the west coast begins. We plan to visit the graves of the Sakalava and Veso Kings, which are near Belo sur Tsiribihina and Marondava. The graves are a tourist attraction because of the sexy wood carvings on the corner posts.

Cowboys in Antsirabe

Werner and Manfred waiting for a Taxi-Bro.

On the way, there is not much traffic. During the rainy season, just like on many other African journeys of late, the road turns into a mud bath and cannot be used. Even during the dry season, only Land Rovers and Mercedes trucks can travel on it. After three hours in Betafo, we manage to cover another twenty kilometres to Soavina. It is a tiny village and has no hotel or restaurant.

But we are lucky, as we meet up with the mayor of the village who invites us into his home for the night. He is a friendly old man with grey hair. My few French sentences help us to communicate. Max and I put our sleeping bags on the boards of a big bed in the centre of the living room. Werner has to sleep on the floor. Dinner is simple, a lot of boiled rice with little stones, harvested from the rice fields around the village. But pieces of meat and fried pork are a true delicacy. Water in which the rice has been boiled is our drink. The leaves of a herb, possibly parsley, have been added and provide some flavour. When we have finished our meal, the family pulls the flat table into the bedroom, and they finish what we have left. Then, we feel bad, as not much is left for them. Our hosts may have to go to bed with almost empty stomachs.

I cannot fall asleep for some time, as I think of times past in South Africa. For more than two years whilst working there, I feel I helped to support a system under which such simple and friendly people are considered inferior; too primitive to even talk to them.

But then, I must have fallen asleep as it is the morning. We discover that the lady of the house is shivering in her bed. It appears she has Malaria and so, we give her a couple of Malaria tablets from our medical kit. I hope they will help.

Around nine o'clock, we hear the noise of a motor. It is the only bus of the day. We run out of the house onto the road and stop it. Meanwhile, Max shakes hands with the mayor and secretly passes some money to him; it is just a small thank you for his generosity. The mayor continues to wave goodbye until we disappear down the road.

We are on our way to Ankazomiriotra; it is a distance of only thirty-six kilometres. Once off the bus, we make our way towards houses that line both sides of the road; and we find some shade under a roof to protect us from the midday sun. A woman accompanies us. She appears to have a mental disease, and her attire is odd as her breasts are hanging out over her dress. A couple of dogs have other worries. Someone offers us cups of coffee and, it makes me wonder, *Would they do that in a central European country?*

Early in the afternoon, a Volkswagen minibus appears. Waving my hand succeeds to pull it over, and we find some room in the back of the bus. The driver, a well-built Malagasy fellow, tells us his destination is Miandrivazo, a distance of 168 kilometres away. That is more than we were hoping for even if we will be travelling not faster than twenty-five kilometres per hour.

By German standards, the road is only a track between agricultural fields. Most of the time, there are rocks instead of soil below the wheels and plenty of bends and shaky wooden bridges. On the way

Photo Above: Studying the map

Photo Left: Sticky problem

down to the coast, some mountain ranges on the edge of the highland have to be passed.

It is late at night when we reach Miandrivazo. The driver of the VW bus does not ask us for money. Later, when I am undressing, I discover that my underwear has a hole at the bottom of the spine surrounded by blood. This has been caused by sitting on a metal bench for which my bum was not designed. Additionally, my rucksack, clothes, and my skin are covered with a thick brown layer of dust. In the small hotel, I pour buckets of water from the Mahajilo River over my head.

CHAPTER 8:

Continuing Travels Around Madagascar

Miandrivazo
20.5.1970

Miandrivazo is a small and boring town. It is also hot, +28ºC at night and up to +40ºC in the daytime. They call that winter here. We decide that we had better keep moving.

A Pakistani merchant sells his goods along the Mahajilo River. He offers to give us a lift in his boat that is made of metal plates that have been welded together. The length of it is about twelve metres with a width of two metres, and the flat bottom is practical because of the shallow water of the river. A canvas roof protects the crew and passengers from the sun. A Malagasy man operates the outboard motor.

It will take some time until we see another shop. To keep the stomachs happy we buy mineral water, bananas and oranges. A couple of casks filled with cooking oil have to be put on board. Three ladies climb in, and we find out that one of them is the cook. Slowly, the boat glides to the middle of the brownish water of the river that

sandbanks have to be avoided. A little breeze cools the air and, the flies stay behind on the beach. The village seems to be their home.

A trip on a tropical river is of special interest for fellows who are only used to lakes and narrow rivers in Europe. Childhood dreams come true, and I think of Tom Sawyer and Huckleberry Fynn and their adventures in a book I have read. The boat slowly travels south around sandbanks, dances on eddies, and, at times, gets pulled along by fast-flowing water. In the distance, on the right side of the river, one can see the steep slopes of the Plateau du Bemaraha through my binoculars. On the left side, we see a mountain range in the distance. But, for now, both sides are flat, and the land is fertile due to the mud and sand of the river. The cosy huts of the Malagasy people are hidden in the shadow of palm trees. On islands, formed by fallen trees and bushes, egrets stand with their long legs; other birds are nearby, also waiting for fish to come closer to their beaks.

The flora and fauna of Madagascar are almost completely different from other countries. I have read that millions of years ago, the big island split from the original continent of Gondwana. Like Australia, with its kangaroos and koalas, it developed along its own lines. One has to be a specialist to understand it all.

Near Tanambao, the Mahajilo and the Mania rivers unite and wind their way through the landscape before they flow into a narrow part of the Indian Ocean called the Mozambique Channel. For a while, we drift along the base of the Bamaraha Mountain Range until we reach an opening. The walls of the mountain on both sides must be up to 200 metres high. From now on, a rain forest covers the land, and the river begins to flow faster.

Slowly, the sun disappears behind the mountain tops painting them in a glowing red and yellow hue. In the fading light, cliffs accompany us for several bends along the river and its untouched natural beauty. Among the treetops, the moon starts rising like

Photo Above: *"Our boat"*

Photo Left: *The kitchen*

Photo Below: *Max crosses the Tsiribihina River*

a distant lantern. To me, this landscape and its beauty are more impressive than the River Rhine with its hills and castles.

Animals whistle and scream among the treetops. Are the native Lemur monkeys competing with the noise of the birds? Suddenly, a shadow effortlessly jumps from one tree to another. Thousands of eyes appear to watch us in the darkness of the night. At the end of the canyon, our "captain" throws a rope around a wooden post in the village of Begidro. It is like waking up from a dream.

A French tobacco farmer welcomes us and invites us into his house for the night. As we settle down, Max tries to catch a little bat in the living room and gets bitten into the finger.

We find out that, once upon a time, there was a car ferry on which one could cross the Tsiribihina River. But for the last ten years, Madagascar has been an independent republic, and so, the remains of the ferry rest and rust on the beach. With the departure of European rule, who will prevent the gnawing of the teeth of time? There is no choice but to cross the river in small outrigger boats and hope that we do not end up in the water with our bags.

On the other bank of the river begins the road to Marondave. Travelling the 106 kilometres in a *Taxi-Brousse* takes two and a half hours over a flat sandy and dry road.

Once we arrive in Marondave, the Hotel Plage has a cheap room for us; by German standards, it is only a small garden cottage. The evening breeze squeezes in through the walls of reeds and looking out, we watch the waves of the Channel of Mozambique roll up onto the white sand of the beach.

When we jump into the water, we surprise a couple of young girls and splash water on them. They are only wearing their undies. We take them off, which they don't seem to mind and invite them for a cool beer in our room. The next day is a well-deserved rest day after the long trip on the river and sandy road.

Marondave
26.5.1970

A new day brings a new adventure. At sunrise, we hop in a taxi and head for the graves of the Vezo Tribe. There are quite a few in the area. But people who have seen most of them prefer the ones which are hard to get to. Our driver knows the way, saying that he has been there many times. A narrow track leads from the main road through thick scrub past huts on cleared land. Our taxi surprises chicken and dogs, which jump aside. Sometimes, our 2CV almost gets stuck on broken termite hills in the middle of the track.

French missionary?

We come across a small lake that is covered with a carpet of blue water roses. As we almost sink into the mud on the beach, we agree that it is time

He is circumcised

to stop. We walk the last 200 metres through the soft sand. Behind a sand dune, the track through the scrub leads down to the coast. On a dune, we find about thirty to forty graves. Graves of the Vezos

The Vezos bury their dead in the ground. There is no sandhill. They build a wooden fence with four or six posts around the flat ground on top of the grave. Modern graves have stone walls. On each post stands a wood carving of the deceased, sometimes a statue of his wife making love and a carving of a bird. I have not studied this religion. But the presence of the wife indicates that life goes on after death. The bird may be a god or totem. We have reached our destination.

The wood carvings on the graves are usually about fifty centimetres high, and due to their age, the wood has cracks. Around the eyes and on other parts of the body, one can often see the original paint. I can't help thinking that the Vezos must have had a happy lifestyle but, even so, some of the love positions on the posts seem to be too acrobatic. Maybe in the other world, bodies are weightless ... It also looks like in death, not only the fingernails and hair keep growing on those wood carvings. Death is not something to be afraid of in this society.

In one of the enclosures, there is a table with a plastic tablecloth, glasses, plates, and cutlery. There is even a flower vase. The dead cannot continue existing by only making love, hence, the crockery and cutlery. It is strange to see a stone cross, too as though being a Christian is only a fashion of modern times to the Vezos. I ponder that perhaps, sitting in paradise, on a cloud, playing the harp, is probably not good enough for them.

We want to visit the second group of graves while there is time left. Halfway back to Belo another track leads us a few kilometres into the scrub. Close to the coast, the vegetation stops and, for about a kilometre, we have to carry our shoes and wade through mud. Sometimes, we unexpectedly sink down to our knees, and it is very slow walking in the midday heat. A lot of crabs that are the size of a man's fist, run around, stand up on their back legs and, with their claws open, threaten us. A bite would definitely hurt and bleed as well. Thorns of fallen tree branches are another obstacle, and I envy our guide with hard skin under his feet.

But, once we arrive, the graves are worth the march through the mud. I use up two Kodak films taking photos of the most interesting carvings. I feel that the censor would stop me from showing them.

Diary of Max, 3.6.1970:

From Marondave, we travel by Taxi-Brousse to the east coast of Madagascar and stay in Mananjary, a small town without a hotel. We make ourselves at home under the shady branches of a tree. Nearby, between the sand dunes, is a small lake. Two naked girls are taking a bath there. Manfred, being a gentleman, offers his towel and asks if he can help dry them. They refuse the offer. But he gets invited for dinner in the hut of one of the girls in a village at a distance of about one and a half kilometres. Werner and I prefer to stay under the tree and take care of Manfred's rucksack.

During the night, the melodic sound of a soft breeze and the waves breaking on the beach nearby is interrupted by the fluttering and crowing of a chicken, on a tree branch above me. It must be having a bad dream as it then almost falls on my head. After this, I pull the sleeping bag over my head, and I hold it closed with my hands. In the morning, Werner and I get up before sunrise and walk along the beach. From far away, we can see hut No. 62 D 4, where Manfred has spent the night with his new girlfriend. Against the light of the rising sun, we see the silhouettes of hundreds of people squatting on the edge of the water. It is the biggest toilet I have ever seen. We agree to reach Manfred's hut by walking along the road further inland.

When we arrive, outside the hut is a crowd of people, at least thirty. They are giggling. Every now and then, someone steps from the crowd and bends down, laughing. They let us pass when we approach. There, we find Manfred, who is wearing only his pants, standing in front of a bowl of water. With the help of his pocket mirror, he tries to pull a razor through the soap in his face.

Manfred continues:

Last night, Christine cooked dinner for me. She placed boiled rice in a bowl and added green leaves. We squatted on a straw mat on the floor and ate with our fingers. She pushed the best leaves to my side of the bowl. We couldn't see the moon because the open door of the hut was blocked by curious onlookers. Maybe, it is the first time that a European has stayed in this village for a night.

Tananarive
7.6.1970

We had planned to travel to Tamatave further up the east coast. But the Pangalanes, a long row of lagoons along this part of the coast, cannot be crossed because of a lack of boats. We return to Tananarive and try to hitch-hike to Tamatave from there. However, there is no traffic. Late in the morning, Max and I take a train to Tamatave. Werner stays behind as he has to return to Johannesburg.

The train ride is slow and shaky along a steep and winding railway line with plenty of tunnels through a rain forest. The French engineers who built this line deserve to be admired. Because of the steep slopes of the valleys, the forest here has not yet been chopped down. Every now and then, one can see waterfalls. When the train stops at villages on the way, one can buy drinks, cooked eggs, cake, biscuits, boiled maniok, and bananas from vendors on the platform. It seems that the whole population of the village has been waiting for the train. It is the highlight of the day. The train seems to take off again only when there have been enough hugs and kisses for departing family members. That's why it takes us until the evening before we arrive in Tamatave.

As usual, we have to find a place where we can sleep and settle down in the cheapest hotel in town. Max and I have to sleep in a single bed. Behind a cardboard wall, which does not reach the ceiling, we hear the owners of the "hotel" snoring, farting, and spitting. Once, we hear the bed squeaking systematically for about ten minutes. Then, the crying baby has to be put on a pot. The cockroaches appear to be tired after searching for food all day and, in a group, they huddle and sleep in the corners of the room. Max takes his sleeping bag and my rain poncho and moves to the concrete strip in front of the house. There he can enjoy the smoke from a heap of rubbish being burnt. When the wind changes direction, it blows some light rain into his face. I finally fall asleep listening to the barking of a dog which is regular, like the sound of a grandfather clock.

Tamatave is a modern and clean town. However, the crumbling plaster on the walls of houses and lots of weeds in front gardens indicate that time has stopped since the French left the country. They had been here for some 100 years.

A wide and straight road lined by palm trees leads to the promenade on the coast. On our third day in Tamatave, I meet Bertine. She seems to like me and invites me to stay in her house, which stands on wooden stilts that move slightly when one walks around on the floor. When I ask where the toilet is, she points to a hole in the living room floor. I had better watch my feet and don't step into it at night!

Max invites her girlfriend to our hotel room. During our last days in Madagascar, we receive tender care. I will never forget the sumptuous food that included a lot of rice, meat and eggs, and crispy pomme frites with which Bertine spoils me. She also has the best-looking body of any of the young ladies I have ever met.

Photo Above: Beach in Northern Madagascar (Postcard)
Photo Right: "Our ship"

After a week, a ship arrives at the wharf. It is the "Pierre Loti" from Marseille, France. It will travel across the Indian Ocean via the French island of Reunion and stop at the island of Mauritius, an independent little country, halfway to India. We plan to fly to Bombay (Mumbai) from Mauritius and explore India by train.

We board the ship and, just before midnight on 13 June, the anchor of the big ship gets pulled up and it slowly makes its way onto the open ocean. The leaves of the palm trees wave a last "Salama tubko" while the lights of Tamatave get smaller and weaker. It is a very sad goodbye. Will I ever see the big red island again?

"Au revoir Madagascar! Malala ti quianau. Je tu n'oublie pas!"

Across the Indian Ocean

The "Pierre Loti" is about 150 metres long and can travel at a speed of seventeen knots, that is thirty kilometres/hour; fast enough for us. Some 200 passengers can sleep in the cabins. Max and I have tickets for the 4th class below the deck. But we prefer fresh air, and so, we sleep on deck. Our beds are a bench and a wooden chest filled with swim vests. My rucksack just fits in, and Max places his bag in a corner behind the box.

I have not slept that long when I wake up because something touches my foot. With the eyes half open, I notice a fellow who tries to hide behind the bench on which Max is sleeping. He is trying to steal Max's bag. At this moment, I regret that I don't know Judo or Karate. I carefully open the zipper of my sleeping bag, take off my socks to avoid slipping on deck, prod Max on his shoulder to wake him up, and jump up from my box. But the thief is faster and manages to run down the stairs into the large bedroom under the deck. I swiftly follow him but, there are doors and beds all over the place. Also, there is no light; I cannot see him. I return to Max, who is glad that he did not lose his bag. We decide to take turns sleeping while we are on the ship.

The next morning, I talk to the maître d'hôtel who is responsible for the 3rd and 4th Classes, and I tell him what happened. I ask

Max and I don't get seasick because we stay on deck.

him to put our luggage into a locker. He hesitates, but finally, he takes our bags into his cabin. Later on, I notice a fellow locked up in a prison cell in the bow of the ship. Someone else must have been faster than I and caught him. A sailor tells me that stealing is normal on board. Some crooks travel 1st Class and have keys for the cabins of the passengers. Max and I agree that sleeping far away from the tourist routes in the huts of the poor people in Madagascar was safer.

A storm comes up. The waves are getting higher and have crowns of white foam. It is hard to walk on deck. When the bow of the ship dips into a wave, some foam flies into my face. One can't see any passengers. They stay under the deck, probably fighting the seasickness. It is my first voyage on a ship, and when I stand or sit, my stomach tries to go on strike. But, I discover that when I lie down in the direction that the ship is travelling, I feel all right.

It takes all day and the next night before we arrive at the island of Reunion. The extinct Volcano Piton du Neige rises 3,000metres into the sky before us. I would love to climb it, but time does not permit it. Only the Fournaise Volcano in the east of the island is still active, although that has not erupted recently. One can notice, immediately, that Reunion is still a colony as the town of Le Port is modern and clean. There is plenty of building activity, and we don't need a visa because, in the middle of the Indian Ocean, we are on French soil. We take a bus to travel the distance of twenty kilometres to the pretty small town of St. Denis. One can really feel the French influence here, although the percentage of mixed-race people is higher here than in France. The island originally was uninhabited, and slaves had to help build the roads and houses.

We make another excursion, this time to the town of St Pierre, and then, we take the last bus back to Le Port. The African-looking driver seems to be new on the job or is drunk as he drives much too fast, passes bus stops where passengers are left behind swearing and, barely misses a fire engine driving towards us on the other side of the

Mountains of the island of Reunion

road. Going around a bend, the driver has to hit the brake to stop the bus a few centimetres before a large rock wall. He continues on the wrong side of the road until some women on board start screaming. At the next stop, many of the passengers get off the bus protesting. We join them, walk a few steps, and stop to wait for a taxi.

Suddenly, a truck appears and comes so close that I quickly step aside and fall into a deep trench. Instinctively, I stretch out my arms as I fall and manage to keep my body above the top of the trench. However, my right foot hits a stone on the bottom, and I hear a crack: a bone on the side of the foot breaks. By the time I am helped out of the trench, my foot has almost doubled in size. A lady from a nearby house brings a chair for me to sit on and a cloth that is wet with medical alcohol. I almost laugh when I remember how Max fell into a hole in Tananarive. That time, he only sprained his foot. Despite the pain, I know that, somehow, I have to return to the ship. By chance, a taxi appears and takes us back fifty kilometres to the ship. It is an expensive goodbye to Reunion. I will be able to claim the money spent from my Allianz travel insurance in Germany. The ship's doctor rubs ointment on my swollen foot and applies a bandage and recommends that I have an x-ray once I arrive in Mauritius. Somewhat helpless, I lie on my chest while Max brings me some food and beer. Climbing the Piton du Neige remains a dream. It seems that once I get to Mauritius I will not be able to do much sightseeing.

The ship arrives in Mauritius the next morning. A police officer in Port Louis counts our travellers cheques because we have no onward air tickets. Max hangs my rucksack in front of his chest and carries his own bag on his shoulder. I hop behind him on one foot to a nearby taxi. It takes us to a hospital where a doctor gives me a needle and some pain killer tablets. He tells me that I need to come back the next day.

Leaving the hospital, we find a clean and comfortable room in the Hotel National. My insurance will pay for the bill. Upon returning to the hospital, they take an x-ray, and once the break is confirmed, they put my foot in plaster, and give me a wooden crutch. For the next ten days, I am either in bed or in an armchair while Max makes a few excursions on his own.

I feel sad. I miss out on the beautiful beaches of Mauritius and maybe some young lady too? With my broken foot, it makes no sense to wait for a ship and so, after some investigation, I find out that every Tuesday, a plane flies out to Bombay (Mumbai). After another three days, we climb into a bus to Mahebourg that is located on the other side of the island. I can carry my rucksack again but limp slowly with the help of a crutch.

The bus trip gives me the only chance to see a bit of the landscape, which, at times, looks almost like the English countryside. Some houses look like English mansions, and there are even some red double-decker buses. The island only gained independence three years ago, and three-quarters of the population are Indians. The remainder are Muslims from Pakistan and some Chinese and Europeans. We are told that since independence, the birth rate, corruption, unemployment, and food prices have continued to increase. The economy is going downhill.

There usually are some Russian "fishing trawlers" in the port. We see one, and it is full of special antennas. Rumours say that the Russians are trying to establish a military base but, so far, have had no luck. It would be in competition with the English Military Base on the nearby island of Diego Garcia.

After our arrival in Mahebourg, we visit a restaurant and rest in the transit hall of the airport. Soon, it is time for us to board our aeroplane, and at 8 pm, the Boeing 707 of Air India takes off. A stewardess serves us a cool beer from the Henninger Brewery in Frankfurt.

One can't fly 4th class like on a ship, and the cost of the air tickets has caused a big hole in our travel budget. We manage to lie down on two empty seats and sleep while we fly some 4,700 kilometres through the night sky, high above the clouds to Bombay.

Church on the island of Mauritius

CHAPTER 9:
India

We land at Santa Cruz Airport in Bombay (Mumbai) early the next morning. The Indian adventure may now begin!

After the controlled air conditioning on the plane, the stinking heat and the humidity of the tropics are almost a shock. When we go to collect our luggage, my rucksack is sitting in a pool of rainwater from the leaking roof, and one of the straps is open. Luckily, nothing is missing, and I think the thief who did this, did not have enough time.

The customs formalities are complicated. Valuables and cash have to be declared and written down. This requirement is necessary in order to avoid black market deals. Intentionally, my binoculars and the 1,500 German Marks inside the cover of my diary don't appear on that list.

On the immigration form, I write Tadj Hotel—the most expensive hotel—as my destination. This avoids having my few travellers' cheques counted which could mean me being sent back to Mauritius. I have no intention of staying at the Tadj Hotel and had already discovered that the YMCA Club seems to be the best deal; the immigration officers do not need to know that.

Signboard

When Max and I walk out from the airport building, we have to get rid of a whole lot of fellows who want to do things for us. I declare that we don't need women or boys, don't want a taxi or to change money. We step into the bus of Air India before the driver of the Tadj Hotel bus can grab our bags. The Air India bus takes us to the YMCA. For a couple of dollars per day, we can put our belongings into a metal cupboard with a lock, have an electric fan, a clean toilet, and a shower.

Max and I explore the city centre and are surprised by the big buildings, wide roads, and squares. The monsoon rain helps to clean the roads but, there is a lot of traffic, and the sidewalks are crowded with people. We find few beggars, pimps, and money changers, and many of the restaurants look inviting. At night, we watch a Bollywood movie in a modern cinema with air conditioning.

In India, alcohol purchases are restricted. Tourists get a voucher for some bottles of beer and a bottle of brandy. That voucher is very popular on the black market. But apart from that, any taxi driver knows where one can buy beer by knocking on a back door somewhere. All this reminds me of my years in Egypt and its black market. I can't help being homesick for Madagascar.

Bombay (Mumbai)
2.7.1970
Sightseeing by taxi does not interest me. But my damaged foot stops me from walking. First, we have a look at the Gateway of India, a large stone arch that was built in 1911 to honour King George V and

Queen Mary. They paid their most valuable colony a visit at the time. Via the Marine Drive along the beach, we reach the Jain Temple. It is reserved for the higher class of society. Under a cupola that is covered with colourful paintings is a square room surrounded by pillars. In openings in the walls sit the statues of various gods which are being worshipped by the believers. Boiled rice and some sweets get offered in order to have some favours done by the gods. We move around among the crowd wearing only our socks—shoes are not permitted—while our guide watches over our shoes.

The next destination is the Towers of Silence, a funeral area for the followers of Zarathustra who worship fire. These followers are not permitted to bury their dead in the ground, and bodies cannot be burned because the fire is holy. According to legend, dead Jains return to the ground through the guts of vultures. The large birds sit in the surrounding palm trees and keep an eye out for new food. The cremation towers are not open to the public. Priests carry the corpses to stone benches and lay them there from which the birds can feed. In the centre of the towers are shafts filled with water. What has been left over by the vultures from their meals gets flushed into the shafts with water hoses. From there, water

"Welcome to India!"

Cyclists in a zoo

pipes lead to deep holes with filters on top, and over the years, the bones turn into mud and finally turn back into the soil.

The funeral rituals of the Hindus are more familiar.

In an open field covered with grass and some rainwater, some blinds of corrugated sheets have been erected. Behind them, a body lies on metal bars and is covered with pieces of wood. The burning wood consumes the corpse and turns it into ashes. Children walk around barefoot in the ashes. It is a Hindu funeral. A funeral attendant adds some more firewood. I wonder, *Do the children watch their grandfather being barbequed? Or is it the corpse of a starved beggar which has been collected by the garbage removalists on the side of a road?*

Back in the taxi, we enter Falkland Road and return to the world of the living. This is the road where widows and other lonely women survive by selling their bodies. From doors, windows, and

Photo Left: Burning a corpse
Photo Below: Vultures at the Tower of Silence waiting for food.

balconies, one can hear happy and laughing voices. They are shouting at us and with gestures that invite us to join them. A pimp is running behind our car, trying to attract our attention. A male prostitute stands at a street corner with a blue dress, shakes his hips, and covers the face with a veil. From a bowl, some dirty water gets splashed over the taxi, a protest against the clicking of the camera.

On the way home, we discover another side of Bombay where poor people live on pieces of cardboard on the footpath. Sheets of cardboard, wood, and corrugated metal lean against house walls. Babies crawl around in the mud, and people make love; they would be better off living as rats or holy cows. I can't help thinking that this dark side of India can be made brighter only by communism.

Prostitutes and customers in Falkland Road, Mumbai

Corruption, the unfulfilled promises of politicians, and the greed of the rich have never done anything good for the underdogs in this world. India's experiment with democracy will have problems competing with their successful neighbour, China. Communist Naxalites in Calcutta are already exploding bombs and killing people. Will the Government of India be able to secure a future of peace and prosperity for its people?

The next day is reserved for an excursion by taxi to the Kanheri Caves in a national park located north of Bombay. On the way, we visit a milk factory. The milk gets collected from the holy cows.

After sterilising the milk, strawberry, or chocolate flavour gets added. No Hindu will drink pure milk from cows that are holy because they are supposed to be the second mothers of the children.

On a highway nearby, which has recently been opened, a whole family of cows rest on the median strip. Some lie in the middle of the road, and trucks drive around them.

As the monsoon rains always start at the same time—just after midday—we make our way back to our rooms. One day we stay dry by visiting the Prince of Wales Museum. My favourite exhibits are in the Tibetan and Nepalese sections.

Express Train to Madras
7.7.1970
The train to Madras on the east coast will cover a distance of 1,340 kilometres and leaves from Victoria Station at 7.50 am. We have reserved seats for 3rd Class. There are wooden bunks on the wall of the cabin which can be folded down, and electric fans make the heat bearable.

Our tickets are cheap because of the 30% difference between the bank rate and the black-market rate. I also travel for the student price because I show my Youth Hostel card with a stamp from the University in Khartoum, in Sudan, where I once stayed for a couple of nights.

The wide railway gauge measures 1.64 metres. On a well-maintained and steep track, the train rolls up to the highland of

New Delhi at night

"Cowboy" on a Highway near Mumbai

Deckan. Unfortunately, we do not see much of the landscape due to the permanent rain. Frequently, the fields on both sides are flooded. A conductor tells us that about every twenty years, the railway line is underwater too. Maybe air cushion trains should be invented?

Along the way, railway platforms are full of life. All sorts of goods are for sale and get advertised with loud voices. Beggars and cripples stick their hands through iron bars on the windows which have been installed to stop people from climbing in … which I used to do in Egypt. That's why the battles at the doors are worse here. Passengers struggle to get to the few available seats. In between, waiters offer railway meals from the station kitchen. The food is wrapped in large green leaves and looks and tastes like the contents of the stomachs of holy cows.

Max and I receive our meals on plates and trays but have to eat with our fingers. We pass the half-finished meals and teacups to the beggars on the platform. Their hands wave in front of our faces while we are eating.

We stick out from the crowd and get asked all sorts of questions: "What your country? What›s your name? Are you married? You have father? You have sister? What your work? You like India? What the time?"

As if time matters in this country! They only understand YES or NO. Children sometimes feel the white skin of my arm and try to rip out a hair.

When we reach the highland, the train stops at Poona, and rice fields stretch out to the horizon. Women in their colourful saris stand in the water in rows, bending down and planting the rice seedlings. At wells, men, children, and buffalos pull buckets up to water the fields. The horns on the grey bodies of the buffalos and their long heads look like question marks. Some buffalos pull ploughs with whips cracking around their ears. This scene has not changed for a thousand years while modern cities in first-world countries are growing and atom bombs are being built.

We pass villages with houses made from mud bricks while palm trees provide shade. Oxen pull carts with heavy loads, and Hindu temples with colourful statues of their gods stand near the villages.

View from the train window

There are mosques and ruins from a distant past. Recently built factories and rows of modern houses look strange in this environment. Farmers who move into the cities become inhabitants of slums. A job in a factory may be easier than working on the land but is not necessarily a guarantee for a better life.

Then, it is night, and we climb into our bunks. Wheels are rolling and rattling, fans are squeaking while they reduce the sweating. From the highland, the train rolls down to the coast. We reach Madras at midday on the following day.

Dense crowds of people fill the streets. We have to push our way through a group of porters, taxi drivers, rickshaw drivers, beggars, and money changers. Outside every railway station in India, one has to cope with this sound barrier of ugliness. While one negotiates the price of the trip by taxi to a cheap hotel, one has to be very careful and look around. Otherwise, a thief may try to rip the watch off a wrist or pull a photo bag from the shoulder of an unsuspecting visitor.

Our scooter-rickshaw is a motorbike in front with a wide bench and two wheels behind. It is a fast and shaky ride with a lot of hooting through the heavy traffic and petrol fumes to the YMCA. We meet a tramp there who had his bag stolen in the community bedroom. This is a reason to look for safer accommodation. Tired and swearing, we decide to make our way down the road and find a room with a lock on the door in the Malaysia Lodge. There is even a ceiling fan and a saltwater shower.

In the Ganga Restaurant, the food is tasty, cheap, vegetarian, and very hot. Madras is known for its spicy dishes. Our eyes are full of tears, and our noses are running. Iced tea seems to evaporate on the way down into our stomachs. We are sweating despite the air conditioning. As I look up at the ceiling, over the edges of gypsum plates, rats look down on us and brush their tails against the lamps. Music from the loudspeakers stops when the electricity fails and leaves us in the dark. The owner of the restaurant turns his torchlight

Circus act in the street in Madras (Chennai)

on every time. The waiters become extra friendly, bend down, and ask if we are enjoying the food. We say yes and start to stand up. Just then, two of the heavy plates fall from above. They break into pieces as they hit the backrests of our seats. Just a split second and a couple of centimetres have us away from hospital beds. We wipe the dust from our shirts, and the manager grabs our hands with a worried face. I explain to him that Lord Krishna, the most important of the gods, has held his hands over us and will keep protecting us.

One of the waiters buys our alcohol licenses for 35 Rupees each. Alcohol is not very healthy in the heat, and we decide that we can be without beer for a while. An Indian whom we know from Bombay invites us for a beer. When he hears that we have lost our licenses in Bombay, he becomes less friendly but buys us a beer with the license of a friend. He tells us that some people pay up to 60 Rupees for the licenses. It seems that the waiter will make a healthy profit when he sells our licenses to someone else. Apparently, one can buy alcohol when a doctor prescribes it for heart disease. I think that Madras must have a large number of people with heart complaints.

10.7.1970

Our "friend" promises to make an excursion with us in the car of his friend. However, he does not show up again. Apparently, he can't make any profit from us, and Max and I agree that, like in Egypt, it is not easy to meet decent and honest people in India.

Once again, we go out to explore the old city of Madras. A group of circus artists performs in the street, and we take photos, and Max records the show on film. Afterwards, we pull a few coins from our pockets to make a donation when suddenly, a whole crowd of begging children surrounds us. The overseer of the circus artists chases them away, and we retreat into a restaurant. He follows us, stands in front of us with a whip in his hands, and demands 10 Rupees; that is far too much. He gets nothing and gets kicked out by the owner of the restaurant. After eating and waiting for a while, we return to our hotel on a cycle rickshaw.

After another couple of days, we decide it is time to move further south. At midday, we sit in a 3rd Class compartment of another express train. Our destination is Ceylon (Sri Lanka). Despite the fan, the heat is almost unbearable. Outside the window, the landscape flies past like a colourful nature film. Even from a train window, India is worth plenty of photos. At railway stations, we drink anything we can buy.

Towns along the way have strange names such as: Madurantakan, Vriddhachalam, Tiruchirappalli, Manapparai. Endless landscapes with palm trees and rice fields always look the same. Only the faces of the people change. Our compartment is open so, Max and I take turns with sleeping to ensure that our bags do not disappear. At Madurai, the sun rises. By 10 am, the train pulls up at the platform in Rameswaram, a fishing village on a peninsula which points to Ceylon. A narrow stretch of the Indian Ocean divides the countries and is connected by Adams Bridge: a chain of rock formations under the water which stretch for thirty kilometres between India and Ceylon. Until the 14th century, it was possible to walk across this.

The formalities at the border are worse than anything I have seen before. We walk around reed huts on the beach and have to fill some forms in twice and sometimes, three times. It is not permitted to export more than 20 Indian Rupees into Ceylon. Surplus Rupees can be deposited at the border, or one can exchange them on the black market nearby for Ceylonese Rupees. Indian banks don't trade with Ceylonese money.

We decide it is best to smuggle the Indian Rupees which we bought on the black market in Bombay and sell them in Colombo for a good profit. It does not pay to be honest in these kinds of countries. In India and Ceylon, one has to declare at the border how much money has been changed in the bank. In Colombo, one can go to a souvenir shop. They put a forged stamp on the relevant form and insert a large amount of US Dollars. Or one can change a small amount in a bank and tell the customs officer that some of his generous countrymen have invited us, and we did not need much money for the whole month. One may give him a few razor blades as a present, and he may buy the wristwatch after retreating to the toilet with his business partner in order not to be seen doing the transaction.

At the wharf, we climb into an old fishing boat that gets pulled by a motorboat. It takes us to "Irwin", an old steamer which, in our opinion, should be dismantled for scrap metal.

It takes "Irwin" four hours to cross the Adams Bridge to a wooden wharf at Talaimannar on the Ceylonese side. Tourists get preferential treatment there. But the red tape still takes a long time. When we get fed up with waiting, we lie down on a bench and pretend to sleep. A customs officer asks us to come to him.

CHAPTER 10:

Ceylon

When I climb onto the train to Colombo, a young fellow does something which is long overdue. He tries to rip my watch from my wrist. But the metal band is tight and does not break. I am still limping and cannot run after him. So, I can only lift my crutch with a threatening gesture. My watch has only a sentimental value; it is very old and has a thin layer of gold on it. It was a present from an uncle of mine who used it for most of his life.

We spend our first night in Ceylon sweating and dreaming in a 2nd Class train cabin.

Colombo
14.7.1970
The train arrives in Colombo in the morning. We find an acceptable room in the CVJM near the railway station. Unfortunately, I spend the day in bed with a throat inflammation and 39C fever. The heat, electric fans, and cold drinks have been too much for my immune system. Strong Penicillin tablets from my medical kit help.

The next day, we try to change money on the black market. I notice some photocopies among the Ceylonese Rupees and put my

Rambodde Tea Estate at Nuwara Elya

money back in my pocket. The "banker" holds my arm and shoulder. Only later do I notice that he managed to pull my 100 Indian Rupee note out from under my handkerchief. Beware of Ceylonese crooks! After this experience, we change money in a souvenir shop at the correct black-market rate. If there were to be any problem, we could return with the police.

When we walk around Colombo, we are impressed with the modern and elegant buildings and parks. It is somewhat similar to Alexandria. But like in Tamatave, I have a feeling that we are walking around in a dying city. Only four months ago, a new government has taken over, which depends largely on Chinese aid and political influence.

Many shop windows are already empty. The import of goods from overseas, especially from the west, has stopped due to the lack of foreign currency. It is the reason for the existence of the black market, an underground economy. There is very little industry in Ceylon apart from the output of tea estates. Trade with the more developed India and its industry is the only way out but, this explains the lower value of the Ceylonese Rupees. Feelings of insecurity are rife among the population. Doctors, engineers, and other educated people are trying to send their savings out of the country and apply for migration to Australia, as well as other countries.

Apparently, corrupt and incapable or lazy governments have followed one after the other. Free schools and free medical care are leaving big holes in the budget. Overseas sales of tea, the main export product, have come to a halt. According to the government propaganda, it is all the fault of the Americans. Pictures of massacres during the Vietnam War decorate house walls. It is no wonder that a few days later, a drunkard calls us "white devils" and wants to spit at Max. In shops, we have to be careful not to pay much more than the correct price.

The Moon Year calendar has been introduced, and in schools, English does not get taught anymore. Tamil, one of the many dialects, is the main business language. This causes friction between the different population groups. A civil war with the Tamil migrants from India looms on the horizon. The future of the island republic is not necessarily a good one.

The monsoon rain and the heat and humidity near the Equator get on our nerves. We climb onto a train destined for Kandy, which is higher up in the mountains. It used to be the capital city until Ceylon became a British colony. Independence came soon after WWII. The train ride into the foothills of the central mountain range takes four hours. Around us is a landscape that looks like a botanical garden. Bundles of coconuts hang from the palm trees. Huts covered with straw roofs get mirrored in the water of rice fields. Cows stop munching the grass between the train rails when the train appears. Colourful parrots scream when they leave the trees, and iguanas with long tails run into hiding. Long-legged herons stand in the water while children have fun in nearby irrigation channels.

Photo Above: *Flowers for sale, an export product*
Photo Top Right: *Sri Lankan "Homebrew"*
Photo Bottom Right: *Curious monkey*
P)hoto Below: *Elephant Bath near Kandy*

At the YMCA Club in Kandy, they have no room for us. We lodge in Castle Hotel. Nearby is a restaurant, and drunk and noisy young Ceylonese make it hard to fall asleep. At night, the landlord places a German shepherd dog on a leash in front of our ground floor room for protection after someone kicks against the door.

Max likes the smell

The rain has followed us from Colombo. We buy umbrellas, and straight away, the rain stops. A bus takes us to the Botanical Garden, which has to be one of the best in the world.

Next is a visit to the Elephant Bath, where work elephants get washed and looked after by their *Mahouts* (overseers) at lunchtime. Max tries to film the scene and slips into the brown water. Only his head and camera stay dry. I am too slow to take a photo of him. He keeps filming until the *Mahouts* pull him out. His passport, vaccination card, and money have to be dried later in our hotel.

Kandy is still too hot for us. We decide to take a bus to Nuwara Eliya, located at an altitude of 1,100 metres in the central highlands. The narrow but sealed road has many bends and beautiful views over the tea plantations where women in colourful dresses pick the ripe tea leaves. Waterfalls drop into deep chasms. When buses come from the opposite direction, the driver has to hit the brakes else, we will follow the waterfalls into the chasms. In Nuwara Eliya, it is finally cool enough to get goosebumps. That is what we want. We only return to Kandy to pick up our bags.

In Nuwara Eliya, we stay in St Andrews Hotel, which is cheap and clean. We are the only guests.

When the British ruled in Ceylon, they built Nuwara Eliya as a holiday resort because of its mild climate and the fertile soil in which they could plant European vegetables. They also planted coffee bushes. When the coffee plants died due to some mysterious disease, tea was planted instead. That was the start of the tea industry, the main export earner of the country.

There is still a golf course, and a horse racing ground and one can also find the red post boxes and phone boots like in England. But the colonial days have gone, and with them, the British ruling class. Few tourists seem to visit the area, and the whole town looks neglected. One can only hope that the economy will recover and make Nuwara Eliya a holiday resort for locals and foreigners again.

The landscape looks almost like Switzerland as, at this altitude, there are few palm trees. Instead, conifers cover the mountain slopes, and cows graze on the meadows which are covered with many colourful flowers.

One can hire boats to explore the local lake. When we wander around in the damp grass on the beach, we encounter a specialty of the town: leeches. They stick to our feet and climb up our legs. By the time we notice them, they fall off because their bellies are swollen and full of our blood. If we were smokers, we could burn them off with a cigarette. We are warned that ripping them out will leave some of the teeth behind in the skin and could cause an infection. When we get home, our underwear is bloody, and it looks like we have had a fight with knives.

I am still limping and cannot follow Max, who climbs a mountain nearby. It is the Pidurutalagala with a height of 2,520 metres. Instead, I take a bus downhill and enjoy a guided tour through the Ramboda Tea Estate. When I try to walk up the hill again, a whole gang of begging children hassle me so much that I climb back onto a bus.

The next day, we visit the Botanical Garden, which is another souvenir of the British days. It has a partly European and partly tropical appearance.

In the afternoon, we take a bus to Banderawela, a village that is even higher and cooler than Nuwara Eliya. We have problems finding the YMCA or other cheap accommodation but, luckily, we meet a man by the name of Dr Anghi, who invites us into his home. He tells us that due to the current economic problems, he will be migrating to Australia with his wife and children in a few months. He has connections to high government officials, which has made it possible to be given an exit permit. We only spend one night with Dr Anghi as we don't want to exploit his hospitality. He drops us off at the YMCA.

We make a trip by bus to Ella. That is not the name of a girlfriend but the name of a village. Nearby is the "Big Gap", from where one can see the coast at a distance of 150 kilometres on a cloudless day.

In a cave is a Buddhist temple. According to Indian mythology, Lord Krishna, the father of the gods, once hid Princess Rana here.

Another Buddhist temple is at Dowa, where a large statue of Buddha has been cut from the rock with chisels some 1,000 years ago.

The next morning, we take a train to Ohiya; this is even higher up in the mountains. It is a beautiful trip along mountainsides, through tunnels, and around many bends with views over valleys full of forests and bushes with colourful blossoms.

Near Ohiya is a footpath to Horton Plains. We have to walk uphill for ten kilometres through rain forests with plenty of birds and butterflies and even monkeys. For my foot, it is the first long march since the accident in Mauritius. Around lunchtime, we reach Farr-Inn, the only accommodation in this area. In the afternoon, we continue our walk through a flora as unusual as it was in Madagascar, and we reach two viewpoints: the Small World's End and the Big World's End. The views are even better than at the Big Gap near Ella. However, it is really cold up here. The lady who runs the hotel spoils us with a hot bath, followed by cold beer by the fireplace and hot water bottles in bed. Unfortunately, she sends the two good-looking female servants home for the next two days. I wonder what she is thinking of … During the night, with the cool air, we sleep like young gods. There are no mosquitoes and only a cold nose and warmth under the blanket. I write in the Guest Book: "It is a perfect place for a honeymoon!"

We stay only for one night and walk back to Ohiya along the fifteen kilometres of sealed road. At night, we are back in Banderawela.

Today is the 30th of July, three months since we left Johannesburg. It does not look like we will get to the World Exhibition in Osaka on time. For now, we have to return to Colombo and change some more money on the black market. The bus travels via Ratnapura, a small town. We watch workers who are busy washing the sand of a river, searching for precious stones. Diamonds and other valuable stones are almost as important for export earnings as tea. Apart from Madagascar and South Africa, there would hardly be another country with more different valuable stones. Heavy rain forces us to continue travelling to Colombo where we fill our wallets again

On 31 July, we keep travelling by train via Maho to Polonnaruwa, an old city full of ruins in the north of Ceylon. We find a cheap hotel owned by an Indian.

The 1st of August happens to be my thirtieth birthday. I celebrate it by buying a bottle of beer for Max.

The Big Gap

It may be of interest to read a bit about the history of Ceylon:

The Sinhalese are related to the South Indian Tamils who have darker skin. But they have always kept separate from the Tamils. This meant that they often had to fight off invaders from India. About 380 years BC, the capital city was Anuradhapura. After 100 years, the son of the Indian Emperor Asoka came to Ceylon with a group of Buddhists. They converted King Devanampiya Tissa. The new religion soon spread all over the country. Several military conquerors followed. Ruling over India was not enough for them. Anuradhapura resisted for 600 years. After its destruction, Polonnaruwa became the new capital. It remained that way for 1,500 years, although, every now and then, an Indian ruler sat on the throne. The third capital was Kandy that the British conquered in 1815. They ruled the country until 1948. Hopefully, independence will not get challenged again in the future.

Polonnruwa is the size of a medium-size German town. With the temperature rising to 40oC, it is rather stressful to wander around among the many ruins. There are quite a few bell-shaped Stupas and Buddha statues showing him meditating in various positions: standing, sitting, lying down. If the big toe is bent, it means that he is not meditating but is dead.

Early in the afternoon, we feel that we have done enough sweating and climb into a bus that transports us to the famous Rock of Sigiria, some forty kilometres from Polonnaruwa. The bench in the back of the bus is loose, and the road has a lot of potholes. Once again, I feel like a cowboy on a wild horse at a rodeo. Other parts of the bus are loose too and make noises like out-of-tune instruments in a concert. At some road crossing, the bus gives up. We have to get out and wait for another bus. In front of a nearby hotel, an American-style limousine is ready to depart. I ask the driver if he is planning to drive past Sigiria. He responds that he will drive along the main road, about six kilometres from Sigiria. That is good enough for us. We put our

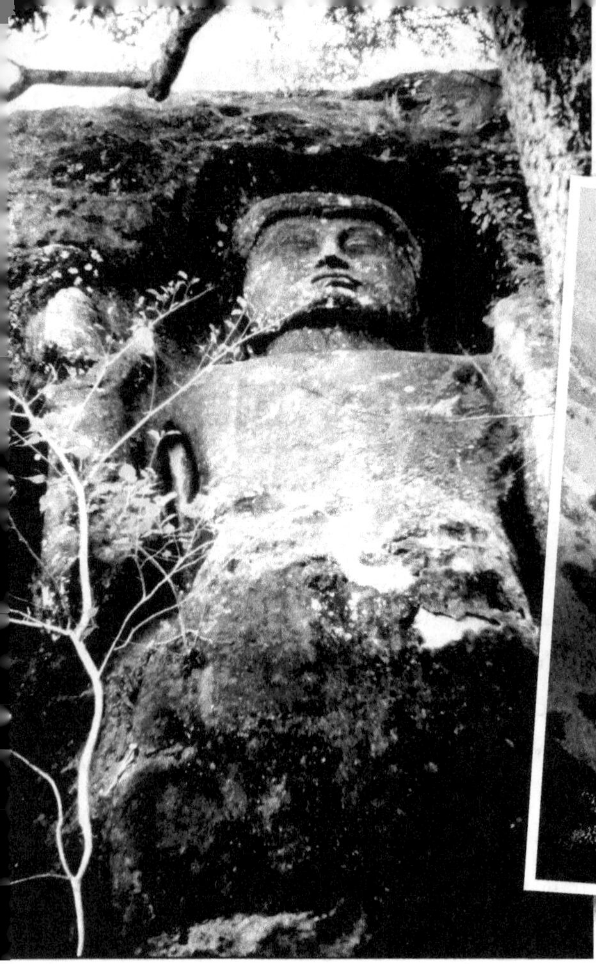

Buddha cut from Rock

View from Big Gap

The Rock of Sygiria

luggage into the boot and sit on soft seats until we reach a crossing where the road to Sigiria begins.

In a mud hut by the side of the road, we drink some coffee and munch a Sri Lanka-style Sinhalese pancake. While we wait for another bus, a herd of work elephants walks past. One of the bulls enjoys playing around with his trunk between the back legs of a female elephant in front of him. As he passes me, he produces a large pool of urine which makes me pull my rucksack away to stop it from getting flooded. Finally, the last bus of the day arrives and takes us to Sigiria. We arrive at sunset and locate the rest house; it is a modern bungalow that reminds me of rest houses in African Nature reserves.

A waiter brings me a special birthday present. He turns the light off and, on a tablet, serves a couple of omelettes which are burning because they have had rum and sugar poured over them and set on fire. Afterwards, we drink Arrack with lemonade. When I go to bed, a large frog sits on the washbasin and watches me with big eyes.

The Rock of Sigiria

The next day is a Sunday. Soon after breakfast, we make our way to the "Lion Rock" and start climbing it. Sinha means lion.

A Sinhalese King called Kassapa became famous because between 473 – 491 he turned the Rock into a fortress and lived on it. Maybe he wanted to live higher than any citizens of his country, a kind of "God King". The history of Sigiria is an interesting study of royal life in the olden days. That is why I will tell it in my own words.

"Once upon the time, there was a king in Anuradhapura by the name of Lanka. He was so cruel and bad that all the people in his country and in neighbouring countries were scared of him. He despised his people so much that once he had a Buddhist monk buried alive because he was meditating in a spot where the engineers of the king wanted to do some work. But this king also had some sons. One of them was called Kassapa. He also had a beautiful daughter. Rich

Photo Above: Manfred on the throne of King Kassapa
Photo Right: Rock painting of servant

people often try to keep their money in the family by committing incest. That's why the princess got married to a nephew of the king.

However, the bridegroom loved the money of his father-in-law more than the princess. He beat her up so often that finally, she ran to her father and told him about her suffering. King Lanka was furious and wondered how he could take revenge on the son-in-law. He finally sent his palace guards to the mother of the nephew and had her burned in public while all the people in the area watched. Horror spread throughout the nation. The nephew came up with his own plot. He persuaded the oldest son of the king to start a revolt. They bribed the soldiers and the leaders of the army. While the population was yelling with joy the cruel King Lanka was arrested and condemned to death. Before he was murdered, he was asked to make a confession. His son asked him where his treasures were hidden because he wanted to be a rich king like his father.

The colours of the rock paintings have faded. I improved them with the computer.

Since the father knew that he was to be killed, he said: "Look, my son, all the treasures I possess are the water canals I have built in the town on which the sun shines and the love of a friend."

After he said that, they ripped his clothes off and put him in chains. With the help of the nephew and the royal cook, a pile of wood was erected. In the meantime, the oldest son killed all his brothers so they could not claim to inherit his throne. When the nephew became worried about his own life, he let the king escape; as he was nude, the cook lent him his underpants.

From then on, Kassapa was worried that his father might return. His guilty conscience bothered him so much that finally, he moved to Sigiria with all his soldiers, priests, and concubines. On top of the Rock of Sigiria, he had a fortress

built with a big throne and three water pools. The top basin was for drinking water. The one in the middle was used to wash the laundry. When the moon was shining, his lovers had fun in the bottom pool while Kassapa sat on his throne and watched them. His painters painted beautiful pictures of his concubines on the walls of the rock. His favourite lover was permitted to prune his beard because not even a barber was allowed to climb the rock.

Some eighteen years passed. The people were happy because the king was in hiding. Rumours had it that he was meditating. But from far away, people came and admired the many beautiful paintings on the rock walls.

Finally, some bad news spread and caused panic. King Lanka had secretly taken his gold from its hiding place and smuggled it to India. There, he hired a large army of mercenaries with long swords and spears. He began to make his way back to Sigiria to take his nephew and Kassapa to court. When the mercenary army arrived, Kassapa climbed from his rock, mounted a large elephant, and rode into battle. However, the elephant stepped in a large hole, broke a leg, and limped away with Kassapa on his back and his trunk between his legs. When the followers of Kassapa saw what happened, they got scared and ran away; the mercenaries chased them. King Lanka spat the juice of a betel nut after his son, destroyed the fortress, and caused horror among the population when he returned to his throne in Anuradhapura. And if he has not died in the meantime, he may still sit there."

After this excursion into the history of Ceylon, it must be mentioned that the Rock of Sigiria is one of the main tourist attractions of Ceylon. One can still climb the rock and sit on the throne of Kassapa. Archaeologists did some digging at the base of the rock and found 1,600 Roman coins from the fifth century before Christ. Was that part of the wages for the mercenaries?

Slum in Mumbai

Trincomalee
2.8.1970

By lunchtime, we sit in a bus again; this time, we are on the way to Trincomalee on the east coast. The trip is rather boring and takes five hours. We arrive at our destination at sunset. After some searching, we find a room in the government Rest House. There is no breeze, and the sweat is running. A bottle of cold beer helps to replace the water in the body. Searching for some cool place, we wander along the beach in the moonshine and lie down in the sand between the fishing boats. Waves gently break on the warm sand. The smell of seaweed and fish hangs in the air under the sparkling stars and the Southern Cross.

Apart from an old fortress and plenty of mosquitoes, we do not find much more of interest and take a taxi to the "Blue Lagoon", a popular spot for excursions. The water is rather shallow. We put on our diving goggles but don't see any coral or water plants or fish. The water is too warm to be refreshing. Disappointed, we return by bus to Anuradhapura and choose a more expensive hotel with an electric ceiling fan, a cold shower, and clean beds with mosquito nets. I need a rest; fleas, mozzies, and the heat have made my bum itchy and sore.

We were planning to return to Kandy for a festival but, we have been told there may be political disturbances. That makes us change our direction.

Ferry to India
6.8.1970
In the afternoon, we take a train to Talaimannar in the north, and stay in the Circuit Bungalow where we enjoy a cool bath in the sea and a clean beach. After that, we feel physically and mentally fit again for another two weeks in India.

At the wharf, the "Irwin" is waiting, the ferry to India. On arrival in Rameswaram, we have to undergo the usual bureaucracy before we can climb into the waiting train to Madras (Chennai).

In the back of my mind, pictures reappear of dirty children with bloated bellies sleeping next to their half-naked parents on pieces of cardboard in the dirt of the street. The lepers whose feet were rotting away crawl after me, begging. Although I was still limping with my crutch, they could not catch up with me.

I can hardly believe that my guts are not yet playing up. But we eat in the best restaurants, enjoy lobsters, king prawns, and crabs, and do not think of the starving people in the slums of India. Spicy food with pepper and chillies is not too hot anymore. Other meals would get stuck in our throats which are dry from the heat.

Due to the many stops, we travel only 570 kilometres in twenty-four hours. In 1916 the train did that in twelve hours. But that was when the British ruled. The dry heat and the rattling train, and a lack of sleep on long train rides are no good for the nerves. In 3rd Class, there are boards on the walls of the cabins which can be folded down. I usually spread my American Army poncho on the floor, push my rucksack under a seat, and put my head on my photo bag. Other passengers put their legs across to the opposite seats. The poncho is necessary because of the red spit of betel nuts on the floor which looks like blood. Beginners think they travel with people who suffer from tuberculosis. Betel nuts produce a feeling of well-being and euphoria and can be addictive. For us, beer is good enough. There is plenty of entertainment on the platforms of the stations. We finally make it to Madras, where we stay in Mohan Lodge for 4 Rupees per night.

Madras (Chennai)
9.8.1970

Today is a Sunday. We should go to church. But churches are hard to find in Hindu India. Instead, we make an excursion on a public bus to Mahabalipuram. Seven impressive pagodas stand near a rock with many steep stairs on which two eagles arrive every day at the same time. They are supposed to fly back and forth between Benares (Varanasi) and this rock. We watch and record the feeding.

Contrary to the eagles, we travel to different destinations. Every night, we decide where we want to sleep the next night. We don't always reach our destination. In between, there are rest days. Our way of travelling can be quite stressful.

India was the Crown Jewel of British colonies. They not only exploited the country, which is really the size of a continent, but also built roads and railway lines and left the English language behind and a democratic form of government. English is a neutral means of communication in a country with a multitude of tribes and nations, with many different languages, cultures, and religions. For Muslims, who are a large minority group, two new states were founded: West and East Pakistan. Populating both required the movement of many millions of people, and because of bad organisation, this cost more than a million lives. Today, India is the largest democratic country. Despite huge economic and plenty of political problems, it slowly progresses and, one day in the future, may become one of the world's most important countries. It is hard to understand how despite a religion with a multitude of gods and rituals, a way into the computer age and scientific achievements can be found.

Diary of Max, 10.8.1970:

At 7.30 am, we catch a train from Madras via Bangalore to Mysore, where we arrive at night. We move into the Ashok Hotel, which is cheap and also find a restaurant with acceptable prices. During the night, up until the morning, I have the runs. More than once per hour, I have to run and later on crawl to the toilet. By the time the sun rises, there is only warm air left in my stomach and guts. And, I have developed a fever as well, reaching 39.4C. In the morning, Manfred looks around for a hospital and finds one that is not far away. When he returns, he pulls one of my arms up over his shoulder and puts his other arm around my body. Then, we slowly limp to the hospital.

The Chief Doctor tells me to stay in hospital for two or three days for observation and treatment. When he confirms that the stay in hospital and the treatment is for free, I agreed to stay. Manfred was told he can spread his sleeping bag on the floor next to me.

Photo Left: Standing on a nail board.
Photo Below: Welcome at the hospital entrance.

We think that is not necessary as it was bad enough that one of us is sick. Manfred is at least vaccinated against Cholera. The room has eighteen beds. One of them becomes mine.
Welcome at the hospital entrance. Standing on a nail board.
With mixed feelings, I take my sandals off and make myself at home on the mattress. Manfred takes off into town to find the medicine which the doctor has prescribed. That, of course, is not free of charge. He also is asked to buy a few green coconuts. The doctor gives me a drip, for which he uses the water of the coconuts to fill my blood vessels and replace the lost liquid. The fibres of coconuts can even be used to stitch wounds caused by war.
The fellow in the bed on my right side helps me to enjoy the environment by looking after me like a mother of a chicken. The student on my left gets spoilt by his family. Two to three times a day, he has about ten visitors at a time around his bed. They feed him with Dr Wanders Ovaltine, Horlicks, and other specialties. But not every patient gets cared for so well. The opposite row of beds has patients who are a lot worse off. They have mostly lung diseases due to malnutrition. All-day long, and especially during the night, one of them starts coughing and groaning until other patients join in with farting and coughing. It is an orchestra that stops me from sleeping.
Twice a day, the skinny patients get cleaned. An assistant puts his arm under the body of the patient and lifts him up while he is holding the blanket with the other hand. This gives a nurse a chance to remove the crap under his bum.
Speaking of nurses! They are like bright lamps in this dark atmosphere. I almost twist my neck muscles when I turn my head to look at them when they walk around between the rows of beds.
Yes, India is a heap of garbage. Manfred and I constantly try to find the raisins in it. Hopefully, in the distant future, things will improve.

Twice during the day and twice during the night, a nurse walks around and measures the pulse and fever. Also, twice a day, the doctor makes a visit. The Chief Doctor comes past once with a whole crowd of junior doctors following him. The patients have to address him as "Sir". Before the doctor arrives, all the visitors have to go into hiding and can come back only after he leaves. No visitors care about visiting times. Some appear carrying a mattress and make themselves at home between the beds for a few days. That makes it hard to distinguish between the sick and healthy people. Some patients sleep on the floor anyway due to the shortage of beds.

Hungry cow "

When I ask a doctor if I can have some of the hospital food, he tells me it is only for the hopeless cases. Ordinary people are not allowed to eat it. Usually, the relatives are

Playboy" in monkey temple

told to bring food for their sick family members. Twice a day, a carer appears with a basket of bread. Even patients who have improved are given a slice. Behind the bread dispenser, a fellow with a can of freshly collected cow milk walks around between the beds and from a ladle pours some of the sweetened and reddish coloured milk into glasses and cups. No Hindu would drink plain *milk from the holy cows. When I ask if there are any tuberculosis bacteria in the uncooked milk, a visitor tells me that Indian cows have no tuberculosis and produce much better milk than the cows in Europe. I doubt that because I have seen them sticking their heads into garbage bins, searching for something edible between dirt, dead rats, and other yucky bits and pieces. Twice a day, a cow and her calf are led into the hospital grounds. First, the calf has to drink in order to clean the "titties", and then the cow gets milked. In my case, instead of cow's milk, I am given sterile coconut milk. Manfred also feeds me with bananas and biscuits.*

I would prefer not to describe the toilets. Every railway toilet in India is cleaner. At eight o'clock in the evening, the water gets turned off. The content of stomachs and guts that is emptied during the night has a tendency to dry and smell until the water gets turned on again in the morning. In the morning, one can see small pools of urine on the floor where it has dribbled through the mattress. One fellow with his skinny legs and arms must have been hungry during the night and emptied the leftover food from the bowl on the small cabinet next to his bed over his head and blanket. Two nurses walk around and straighten the bedsheets. It permits a glimpse at the mattresses which have a lot of yellow rings indicating the age of the mattresses.

The holes in the floor show where the bathtub must have stood. On the wall is a boiler which actually works except that the tap is missing. There also is a petrol drum with the top cut off. "Dust Bin" is written on it. From a pipe in the wall, water runs into it. It seems to be rainwater which gets collected in the cellar. Pumps distribute it to the various bathrooms.

Suddenly, a crow flies in through the open windows and, after a few rounds around the room, settles on a lampshade hanging under the ceiling. The old crow has a look around at all the bits and pieces of food on plates and on the floor. Some patients do not like to see the bird and wave their skinny arms in the air. The crow regards this as a greeting and lands on a bed frame. There it sharpens its beak and empties its guts. Then it jumps on the floor and gets stuck into a split bowl of mutton curry until a male nurse comes running and chases the crow away. It takes off with a big piece of meat in its beak and, due to a sudden bend of the corridor on the way out, almost hits the wall with its wings.

The staff of the hospital fulfil their duty as best as possible, and no patient receives special treatment. One of my favourite nurses receives my last "Life Boy" soap after I lent it to her a few times. The soap is a luxury not available in the hospital.

After a couple of days, my legs feel stronger, and I can walk again. Manfred collects me on the morning of 13th August. He is accompanied by Vreni and Ursina, two Swiss girls who have tramped from West Africa through Tschad to Sudan and India and are on their way to Australia. It is very unusual for girls to do such trips.

Waiting for a train.

The next day, at midday, we take a train to Arsikere where we change onto a train to Poona. From there, an express train takes us to Bombay (Mumbai); a journey of thirty-three hours.

The next day is a Sunday. A taxi driver with the number 746 on his uniform has changed some money for us to keep us going to Nepal. The Cholera was free of charge.

17.8.1970

After a day of rest, we take an express train to Aurangabad, where we arrive at 4 pm and move into Café Vinhoo for 3 Rupees per person per night.

The next day, we make an excursion to the Rock Temples of Ellora, which were completed more than 1,000 years ago. Details about Ellora can be found on the Internet. In the afternoon, a bus takes us to Ajanta, where we arrive late in the evening. In a Government Bungalow, they have two beds for us for 2.50 Rupees per night. We are very happy to be able to take a shower and have a good sleep. In Ellora, it was raining, and we were walking around in mud all day.

Our Rest House has built only three years ago. It is clean and well maintained. There is a front garden with a fountain; and our two beds have clean bedsheets and bed covers, mosquito nets, and electric fans on the ceiling. The bathroom and showers are clean too, and the water keeps running all day. Such moments are medicine for the soul because of our way of travelling.

The next morning, Max measures his temperature, and with 38.1C, has quite a fever, possibly a result of our walking in the rain and some cool wind on the wet clothes. We decide to rest for another day while it is raining cats and dogs. While Max is sleeping, I make an excursion to the caves of Ajanta on my own. My umbrella gives me limited protection against the rain. The Ajanta Caves are worth a look on the Internet.

Camera demonstration

By Thursday, Max has recovered. Early in the morning, we climb into the "Amritsar" Express, which takes us to Agra. We arrive there at 2.30 am during the night. Some cycle rickshaw drivers ask for too much money to take us into town. We decide to walk along the dark road with our heavy packs on our shoulders while the rickshaw drivers start reducing their fares. After about two kilometres, we find a garage with some light from a lamp and spread our sleeping bags on a concrete floor for the rest of the night. The concrete is still warm after the sunshine during the day.

We have saved the money for the stay in a hotel, and after a while, we find the Agra Hotel and a room and enjoy a breakfast

Temple of Ellora

with a cool beer, eggs, toast, and tea. It gives us enough energy for a sightseeing trip on a bus to the empty ghost town of Fatehpur Sikri. This abandoned city can be studied under Wikipedia on the Internet.

Our next destination is the Red Fort. It takes a few hours to explore the rooms and fortifications. The history of the fort has been written down in Wikipedia. The mosque within the fort has been built with white marble tiles and reflects the sun. Max has taken off his sandals and keeps dancing with closed eyes and a dried-out throat on the hot tiles of the floor around the fort. He finally finds a stand where they sell Coca-Cola. Max reaches into the icebox and throws a few hands full of ice water into his face. He drinks a bottle of Coke nonstop. Our bus does not wait for us and took off.

We still have to walk a mile to the Taj Mahal. It contains the grave of an Indian princess and is one of the most famous buildings in the world. But the local and international tourist groups are annoying with their noise and shouting. They try to check the echo in the huge room where the two marble coffins stand in the centre. Some tourists even bang on the lids of the coffins to find out if they are about to

Tadj Mahal in the evening

The Golden Temple and its holy lake in Amritsar. Head Office of the Sikh religion.

break or perhaps, there is some other reason that they kick the coffins with their shoes … We don't see any guards or police.

All around this tourist attraction, children are located amongst the crowds. They stretch out their hands and ask for *baksheesh* (money).

The outer walls of the Taj Mahal used to be inlaid with precious stones. Sadly, most of them are missing. An Indian tells us they were stolen by British soldiers. I suspect it was locals rather than an international robbery.

It has been one of the hottest days of our trip, with up to 45C. In the evening, the tourists disappear. We lie on the grass and enjoy the sunset behind the Taj Mahal. The moon does not shine yet, and we watch as children run across the flower beds and play hide and seek behind the bushes. Young lovers stroll around and listen to loud music from their radios. We don't stay long and are still upset about the humiliating treatment of a beautiful monument which is in actual fact, a grave. Soon we are back in the Agra Hotel.

Taking a bath in the holy lake.

On 22 August, we take an express train to New Delhi, the most glamorous and most expensive city of India; it is the capital. In the YMCA Tourist Hotel, they charge us 20 Rupees per night. At least it includes breakfast. This is the most expensive accommodation that we have to pay for in India. Of course, there also are the bigger and much more expensive hotels. But we only go to visit those to change some travellers' cheques or pinch toilet paper which is hard to find in India. In Indian toilets, there are water cans next to holes in the floor. The left hand is "unclean" and does not get used to eating. We use both systems and usually eat with a spoon and fork. Other countries, other customs …

Oh, India! Yesterday stones were flying after us in retribution as Max smacked a young beggar's face after he spat him on the cheek. Many people annoy us by asking stupid questions or trying to sell us something. Still, there are photo opportunities all around us. But moving around on foot among the crowds of people sometimes frays our nerves more than it did in Egypt. There probably exists a

Reading from the Guru Granth Sahib.

different India, but this can only be experienced if one rides a bicycle through the countryside from village to village. This is a trip I may try in my next life.

The air of New Delhi is full of dust that hangs in the hot and humid air combined with the fumes of millions of cars. Max still has a cold and keeps coughing all the time. We don't want to stay in this unhealthy environment and apply for tourist visas for Nepal.

Feeding time in the monkey temple.

On 26 August, the Mail Express leaves on time at 9.15 pm, in the evening. After a night ride of eleven hours, we reach Amritsar the next morning. This is the home of the Golden Temple of the Sikhs. They are people who look different from others because they have a beard and wear turbans. The Golden Temple is the Vatican of the Sikhs, a holy building standing in an artificial lake. According to legend, bathing in the lake cleans away all sins. Yet, I wonder with a smirk, *How many bacteria does it add to the body?*

The roof of the main building (Gudwara) is covered with gold leaf. This is the place where the Holy Book gets read without a break. Visitors pray.

The Sikh Religion was founded more than 500 years ago by Guru Nanak, a holy man. We would call him a philosopher or prophet.

This religion is open-minded and has aspects of Christian and Muslim religions. There is only one god, and he looks after the people of all religions. Travellers of any background or religion find free accommodation in the temple premises; it is a generous offer that we have often accepted in East Africa. That is the reason why the Golden Temple is my main attraction in India.

There are about 20 million Sikhs in India. They often have a good education and can be found in important positions in the government and especially in the army.

In the evening, we sit on rolling wheels again in the Varanasi (Benares) Mail Express train that is heading towards Nepal. We travel through the night and most of the day until, at 6 pm, we arrive in Varanasi, the correct name for Benares.

In the Benares Lodge, they have a room for us. We reside in the old romantic part of town with narrow lanes and old houses where holy cows, human beings, rats, dogs, cockroaches, and many other living things share the dusty footpath. Next to a police station, a little lane leads into the darkness. This is where the prostitutes reside and run their horizontal trade. Despite all of this, Varanasi is quite an impressive town. It is one of the oldest in the world and is considered the holy city for the Hindus, like Jerusalem is for the Christians and Mecca for the Muslims. The streets and parks are rather clean by Indian standards. We see few beggars and crippled people.

We make a short trip by boat on the river Ganges and have a look at the Burning Ghats, where corpses in the Hindu tradition get burnt in wood fires. Sometimes, there seems to be a shortage of wood, and we find out that this is the case because every now and then, a bloated corpse drifts down the river with crows sitting on it and pulling out the guts. Colourful and romantic India!

Another tourist attraction is the Monkey Temple, an important temple for Hindus. The many monkeys are not holy but, for some reason, are tolerated. They are not shy and do not hesitate to search our pockets for peanuts which one can buy in the temple for feeding the monkeys.

30.8.1970

It is time to depart from India. At 2 pm, we take a train to Mogul Serail where we have to change for a 4 pm express train to Patna on the southern side of the Ganges River. An old paddle-steamer from the British days called "Gomati" takes us to the northern side of the river. That journey takes two hours. The town on this bank of the Ganges is called Palezabat. Another train ends in Muzaffarpur from where a slow old train takes off to Sagauli. Finally, we travel in the very last train to Raxoul. This is the town located at the border of Nepal. After a total travel time of twenty-four hours, we are quite exhausted. In between, we could not sleep and had to watch our bags. We could not buy much food, and there were no hot drinks either. It is dangerous to drink water that has not been boiled. Max has had Cholera once already; he does not want to catch it again.

CHAPTER 11: '

The Road to Kathmandu

The road to Kathmandu

Diary of Max, 31.8.1970:

During the last train ride in 3rd class, on the way to Raxoul, most passengers get off at different stations. The remaining travellers who plan to cross the border sleep on the luggage rails. Manfred and a French hippie, who is also on the way to Kathmandu, sit on the floor together in the open door with their legs hanging outside, trying to have a conversation. The hippie talks the most because Manfred only knows a few words of French. They are enjoying the fresh evening air but, when the wind suddenly changes direction, the smoke of the steam locomotive envelops them, and I can hear them coughing and gasping for air.

I spy an empty wooden bench and lie down to sleep on it. When we reach Raxoul, Manfred wakes me up. The hippie with his long hair looks like the second edition of Jesus and has a disgusted expression on his face as he points at the Indian who is sleeping on the wooden rails on top of me. That person appears to be suffering from some

Changing a tyre on the way to Kathmandu

form of leprosy! He has various sores on his rotting feet from where a greenish liquid emerges, forming long strands. This green puss has turned into droplets that have fallen into my hair and onto the jacket of my safari suit. As this has taken place during the night, the result is that I look a bit slimy. It is disgusting! When we move into the government Rest House in Raxoul, I disappear into the bathroom and start a major washing and rinsing operation.

Manfred writes:

In the morning, we pass through the border formalities without a problem. A waiting bus takes off, with us in it, on the long road to Kathmandu, the capital of Nepal. It is an unsealed road with many bends and potholes which leads up into the foothills of the Himalaya Mountain Range. It would be hard to build railway lines in this environment. On the way, the bus develops a flat tyre. It takes a long time to replace the wheel. The hills at this point become so steep that the bus can only travel in first gear. Further, it has to carefully navigate a few narrow stretches where a part of the road has been washed away into the 800-metre-deep valley.

In one of the bends, a hole in the clouds reveals Mount Everest that is 150 kilometres away. The light of the evening sun gets reflected from the ice on the majestic summit. At the next corner, Mount Everest appears again. On the left side of it, one can see the Annapurna and the Dhaulagiri Mountain Range. Some of the passengers hang their heads out of the window and are sick. People sitting behind them have to be careful not to get sprayed.

In a very narrow and steep bend, the gearbox starts making metallic music. Another bus from the same company has to stop and exchange passengers with our bus. Now the old bus can roll downhill to make it easy for the damaged motor. Finally, at 2,000metres, we reach a mountain pass and roll into the Kathmandu valley. We arrive in Kathmandu at 8 pm.

In the Merina Hotel we insist on having our own room. From the community bedroom we can smell the smoke of marihuana which makes the hippies dream.

Mount Everest

Kathmandu
2.9.1970

After visiting Nepal, we would love to travel to Lhasa in Tibet to climb to the top of the Potala, the palace of the Dalai Lama. But, at the Chinese Embassy, our visa application gets refused due to the missing diplomatic relations between Germany, Switzerland and China. The real reasons are probably the political tension and military activities of China in Tibet.

Kathmandu, due to its age and romantic atmosphere, has to be the most fascinating city on our trip. It spreads out at the height of 1,500metres in a green valley that is surrounded by medium mountain ranges and the tallest peaks of the world in the background. The city has preserved the streets and houses of the Middle Ages and some of the lifestyle too. It is a paradise for hippies who want to escape the formalities and stress of the Western World. But when the money is finished, and the smoke of the marihuana has disappeared, they have to return home and maybe improve their education and do some job training.

Max and I may have left Europe for similar reasons but, but we are aware that one has to work for a living. One can only save as much money as possible and enjoy unemployment for a few dollars a day in poor countries until it is time to work again. We may be lucky and end up in a country like Australia or New Zealand, where an easy lifestyle exists despite a lot of work. Life is a compromise!

The heat, dust, humidity, and stench of sweat and car fumes in India are forgotten. We shortened our stay in India by at least two weeks to rather travel here. Up here, the mountain sun burns our faces. When the wind in the afternoon blows black clouds against the mountain tops, a cool rain starts falling. The wind brings with it the smell of trees, grass, and rice fields.

Kathmandu has about 500,000 inhabitants; it is a truly international mixture. The reason may be that Nepal is a buffer state

Nepalese Gods

Streets of Kathmandu

Wood carvings on Temple walls. Education for children?

between India and Tibet which belongs to China. People from all three countries have mixed here over hundreds of years. The majority have Asiatic faces with slit eyes, strong cheekbones, and faces burnt brown by the sun, and wrinkles caused by a hard-working life. In between these, are Indians and Tibetan refugees who have escaped the killing spree of the Chinese. There are also tourists from Europe, mainly with long hair, neglected, skinny, and dressed as clowns. They make the Nepalese laugh and sometimes feel sorry but, in the Asian way, they tolerate these strangers. After all, they bring some foreign currency and buy the locally produced marihuana.

The Nepalese follow a local form of Hinduism and seem to have some colourful gods whose statues they worship in the streets. The streets still have the old houses that are seldom interrupted by a new one. Most of the roads have been sealed and seem to get cleaned regularly. There are not many cars, but a lot of bicycles and cycle rickshaws. Because of the narrow streets, there is a permanent concert of bicycle bells and the hooting of cars that is an imitation of large cities. One can enter a side street without traffic, and suddenly, life is like it has always been. The houses have pointed roofs made of tiles and sometimes lean against each other for support. Small shops offer their goods, and family life extends onto the street.

Everywhere are wood carvings: they are situated on doors, windows, balconies, and supporting beams of roofs. They show ornaments, flowers, animals, gods and lovers. The fairy tale world of Hinduism has mixed with the local beliefs. Then there are the temples: at many streets corners and in many squares. Pagodas with two floors rise above the houses and the sun gets reflected by roofs made of sheets of copper, zinc, or metal plates covered with gold leaf. Eyes have been painted on temple walls symbolising the presence of gods which watch over the actions of the believers. Those actions can be quite intimate …

Bagmati River. Women washing their sins away.

One believer kisses the stone feet of the god of horror with its many arms. In front of Hanuman, the Monkey God, the lights of butter lamps are flickering.

Siwa, the strict god with three faces, has flower garlands hanging around her neck. Finally, in the courtyard of the Pashupatinath Temple, we find a huge golden calf, maybe a Nepalese statue of a holy cow. Moses would be interested in that calf. You can refer to the Old Testament for more on this.

2.9.1970

Today is the Taj Brata Festival, a kind of Mother's Day for Hindus. It lasts for three days. And women from all over the Kathmandu valley come to Kathmandu. They wear their best saris, of which many are red. Others are yellow or are decorated with colourful threads and made of silk. Hea scarves flutter in the wind. The crowd of pilgrims walks to the Bagmati River; it is as holy in Nepal as the Ganges in India, into which it flows. Due to the rainy season, the water is grey and muddy and rushes past the steps of a temple. There the women throw colourful blossoms into the water and take a ritual bath.

We spend a few more days exploring Kathmandu and buy some souvenirs. With hired bicycles, we make an excursion into the surrounding countryside, meet friendly people, and do not get hassled by begging children.

A bus takes us to the mountain pass at Daman at an altitude of 2,325 metres. From there, one can get a first-class view of Mount Everest. We stay in the Mansarovar Hotel because we want to film and take photos of the mountains in the morning.

After returning to Kathmandu, we buy air tickets to Bangkok (Krung Thep) in Thailand.

There is still time, though for a visit to the small town of Badgaon, at a distance of ten kilometres from Kathmandu. A European town would have looked like this during the middle ages as cobblestones cover streets and squares have water-wells in the centre.

Copper kettles hang on ropes that run over wheels. Barefooted girls pull the full kettles from a depth of thirty metres. Pigs roll around in the dirty water of drainage channels which children use as toilets

Himalaya Mountains

Photo Above: Traditional transport

Photo Left: The "Goddess" Kumari

Photo Below Left: Badgaon

Photo Below Right: The Shwedagon Pagoda (Postcard

in the daytime. Adults only do that at night. No telegraph wires or other electric cables disfigure these romantic-looking streets. In schools, children and teachers sit cross-legged on the floor in rooms that are open to the street. The children yell and scream at us and wave their writing slates. Few tourists or other foreigners appear to visit this town.

It is sad to look at a group of porters carrying their loads to the base camp of K2, which is 8,610 metres high, as we would like to follow them to the base camp. But, the slowly healing foot of mine (Manfred) makes it impossible.

Our plane to Kathmandu almost takes off without Max because he walks to the end of the runway to record the departure of the first plane. It is important for the planes to leave as early as possible because cloud banks soon cover the mountain tops and endanger the planes which fly over them.

Nepal seems to have more festivals than any other country. On 14 September, the Goddess of Kumari gets honoured. She is only four years old. It appears a bit strange to our European minds. Every four years, a young girl who has not yet reached puberty and who belongs to the upper class gets declared a goddess.

Honouring the child is a manifestation of the god-given female energy, referring probably to women giving life to their children. Kumari gets painted with lipsticks and gets dressed in valuable costumes. She sits on a large decorated wooden cart with big wheels, which gets pulled along the roads by a group of men. Crowds of onlookers watch and admire the goddess and wave and cheer.

15.9.1970

We have plenty of time but a very limited travel budget. It is with regret that we leave Nepal and move a bit further east on the world map. Travelling overland seems to be insecure as in the rainy season, the flat areas behind Calcutta like Bengal, Assam, and East Pakistan

A message of peace

A gold plated Buddha

are partly flooded. Apparently, a lot of people have drowned in those areas, and thousands of mud-brick houses have been washed away.

It is hard to tell if the border of Burma (Myanmar) is open because of civil war activities in the area. It leaves us no choice but to step into a Turboprop Vickers Viscount plane of Burma Airlines. After a stopover in Dacca, we land in Rangoon (Yangon), Burma (Myanmar), at 6 pm, in the evening. We are lucky to find a room in the local YMCA.

Burma used to be a British colony and, after independence in 1948, it became isolated from the outside world by a military dictatorship. Officially, it is a Socialist Republic. But there are communist uprisings in the northern and eastern provinces. Our visa does not permit us to travel inland. We have to stay in Rangoon and only for one week. The traffic seems to have changed little since 1948. There are few

Photo Left: Market stall
Photo Top: Shop on the river
Photo Below: Floating market in Bangkok (Postcard)

private cars on the roads, but a lot of military vehicles from different donor countries like Russia and China; they are a museum on wheels. The shop windows are empty.

We have problems trying to find something to eat. There are only a few clean restaurants, and they are expensive. Small shops, where the sweet juice gets pressed from sugarcane, are the best culinary attraction. Enriched with some lemon juice, it is a refreshing drink in the tropical heat. In one restaurant, we finally obtain a plate of noodles with vegetables and some chicken pieces for an acceptable price. One cannot buy milk, butter, or potatoes, and bread is almost impossible to eat. Okay, we are in a country where rice is the staple food.

The main attraction in Rangoon is the golden Shwedagon Pagoda. We notice a group of men who sit on the floor in a circle and

Photo Above: Alan Simpson and Max

Photo Right: Temple snake

Photo Below: Yummy fish for sale

hold up a model sailing ship. One of them explains to us that, once a week, they come here in a group to pray. The ship is supposed to send a message of peace around the world. I tell them that, unfortunately, there is no chance for peace as long as too many generals rule the world. It is a hint at their own government. The image of that ship will sail with me until the end of my days.

As we walk around, we notice that the people are clean and friendly and often have a high school education as they speak English fluently. They approach us and complain about their fate and Socialism. They tell us about the good times during Colonialism and complain about dictatorship and the policy of scarcity. Like in Ceylon, the independence between the power games of East and West comes at a high price. Tourists are well-advised to visit other countries.

After only one day in Rangoon, we again avoid travelling by road through the countryside where bullets may zoom through the air. We arrive in Bangkok (Krung Thep), the capital of Thailand, after a flight of only one hour. There is no problem at Customs Control. But, an American Officer checks our passports before he passes them on to a Thai official. This may happen because the American Army is stationed here and is fighting the Vietcong in neighbouring Vietnam.

After Rangoon, it is a civilisation shock to look at Bangkok. It is amazing how the might of the dollar can change the world. A private bus takes us at a high speed along the ten kilometres long modern highway to the city. Despite the heavy traffic, there is none of the slow and disorganised traffic of other Asian countries. There is no room for cows and goats on the roads and on the footpaths. No snake charmers and magicians attract a crowd and slow down the traffic. *And why is that so?* Ordinary people have jobs. The economy is booming thanks to the war in Vietnam. Bangkok is like an oasis where the soldiers can relax after the horrors of the war. The city is a supply base for the troops in Vietnam. There is not much industry in the country. Trading of all sorts of goods happens mainly in Bangkok. European

Photo Above: Djakarta
Photo Left: Unusual load
Photo Below: Shoe shine boy

companies are permitted to do business in Thailand and make good profits from the war. Blood gets turned into money.

We are delighted to find that there are still floating markets on the rivers and canals. One can find hotels of all kinds which often are very expensive. Even the Atlanta Hotel, which we find, after searching for it for two days, is clean and cheap and has a swimming pool. It also has a good and cheap restaurant for us. There are hundreds of clean and modern restaurants with tasty food in Bangkok where even choosy guests can spoil their stomachs.

In between, one can stand in front of shop windows where twenty to thirty girls with numbers on their uniforms and, who are between the ages of twenty and thirty years old, sit smiling on wooden benches. The sign on top of the window advertises "Turkish Bath Massage Salon". At the cash register at the entrance, one only has to mention the desired number. Then, one of the beauties appears with a towel and a bottle of Coca-Cola in one hand, and an alarm clock in the other, and leads the guest up some stairs to a workroom. Every minute counts. All limbs from head to toe get massaged, hard ones will be softened with a special method if requested, which is strange for this institute. But so far, no one has complained.

After sunset, all over the city, neon lamps in a multitude of colours cover walls and open spaces and turn the night into a flickering spectacle. Now, the nightlife begins. Most restaurants are open for twenty-four hours. Large and modern cinemas show the latest movies from the United States. The sex industry is in full swing. Hotels offer international shows like folk dance groups or a Munich-style Oktoberfest. My new girlfriend has lived in Germany, gives me a red rose as a present and puts on her dirndl dress when I take her to the movies. Max prefers to stay in our hotel room with Dhaji, who is only sixteen years old.

On 20 September, we make an excursion by boat on the Chao Praya River to Ayuttaya, an old temple city that is partly overgrown by the jungle. The Stupas look like towers and often contain the remains of Buddhist monks. In Bangkok, we start looking for work, not because we need money, but because we like the lifestyle. Unfortunately, none of the German or Swiss companies needs us. But the Manager of the German Chamber of Commerce at least invites us to a nightclub. The Goethe Institute and the Thai-German Cultural Society take us along in their buses on sightseeing tours. After the long dry spell between Madagascar and Thailand, we enjoy this life of luxury for two weeks before it is time to move on.

On 30 September, we leave on an express train to Malaysia in the south and stopover for a night in the Haul HinLarug Hotel in Hua Hin, a small town. In the morning, we board a rapid train to Surat Thani. It takes all day to get there. A hotel is next to the railway station.

Another day gets spent on a slow train to Nakhon Si Tammarat on the east coast of the Malayan peninsula. It is a holiday resort, and all the hotels are fully booked. We have no choice but to rent a room with a big bed in the local brothel. A police officer must wonder what two fellows are doing in a bed together in this establishment and he knocks on our door in the middle of the night to check our passports.

The train connections are a bit confusing and, in the morning, we travel back to Khao Chum Thong and climb onto an express train. Yesterday, we sat in a part of the train which was redirected in Haad Yai to Sonkhla. The other part of the train was pulled to Padang Besar by a new locomotive. We keep swearing while we return to Haad Yai where we finally step onto a local train to Padang Besar. After one hour, we arrive at the border of Malaysia.

On 4 October, we pass through Customs Control and take a train to Butterworth where we arrive at 10 pm. A ferry floats across to Georgetown on the island of Penang and, in the Lum Fong Hotel, they have a room for us three.

On the way to Penang, we meet Alan Simpson, a tramp from Coventry in England. We decide to continue our journey together. A cable car takes us to the top of the 800-metre-high Penang Hill, which permits a beautiful view over the island and Georgetown. The lifestyle here is much stricter than in Bangkok. It makes us concentrate more on the beauty of the natural surroundings. There do not seem to be any churches here. But we visit a Snake Temple. This appears different from the days of Adam and Eve as these snakes do not 'speak' and they seem to be sleepy from the smell of the incense sticks around them. There is no apple tree in the yard on which they could rest, and one of the snakes is happy to hang around my neck. Markets offer plenty of fish fillets with which to feed them.

The next stopover is Kuala Lumpur, the capital of Malaysia. It takes all day to get there in an express train. After some bargaining, the three of us move into a two-bedroomed room for 2 US dollars per night. As soon as we move in, three girls appear at the door and want to move in too at a price of US$13. The owner of the hotel would probably receive a share. We reject the offer and spend the money in a restaurant.

While we have a look around town, Max and I also try to find work. But a large German Civil Engineering firm which enlarges the harbour docks cannot employ us. The government is very strict and does not allow foreigners to work here. In Egypt, one could bypass the rules with a handsome *baksheesh*.

We spend another two days with bureaucracy, sightseeing, and a visit to a cinema. The title of the movie is *The Adventurers – Civil Wars in South America*. Bypassing Singapore, we fly to Pakembaru that is located on the island of Sumatra in Indonesia with a Fokker Friendship plane of Air Garuda. Despite many years under colonial rule by the Dutch, the country is still not very developed. The people are mostly poor and can be rather nasty and aggressive. We continue on a bus and stop at a river where we wait for four hours for a ferry.

There used to be a bridge here once, but now, only a couple of pillars stick out from the water. It takes fifteen hours to get to Padang. I make an excursion with Alan while Max rests in Hotel Mariani.

On 21 October, another Fokker Friendship flies to Djakarta via Palembang. Djakarta is the capital of Indonesia on the western end of the island of Java. Heavy monsoon rain is pouring down on us. We take two cycle rickshaws into town and lose Max on the way. I end up in a Youth Hostel with Alan. It would be a disaster if we could not find Max again in this huge city. But Max and I have the same thinking, and on the next morning, we ring the Swiss Embassy and are happy to be reunited. Max ended up in the army barracks where an Anti-tank Battalion resides. The Sergeant Major invited him to spend the night in an army bed.

A lot of time gets wasted when we have to stay too long in the city waiting for a visa to enter the next country, in this case, Australia. It takes five days before it is approved. By now, we have forgotten the World Exhibition in Osaka. We spend the time tramping on a truck to Pelabuanratu on the south coast of Java. It is a little fishing village in idyllic surroundings.

After a night in a cheap hotel, we return to Djakarta to look around the city and, once again, visit a cinema.

Early in the afternoon, on 27 October, a train takes us to Bandung. Hotel Lugina is affiliated with the Youth Hostel Association and costs only a few dollars.

In the vicinity is the 1,800-metre-high volcano, Takubanprah, with a steaming

crater lake. From the bus stop, we get a lift to the edge of the crater. Despite a warning of sudden eruptions, we climb into the crater to take close-up photos of the sulphuric steam coming from holes in the wall. We keep well away from the thin crust at the edge of the lake and climb back up before the steam damages our lungs. Japanese tourists drive us back to Bandung.

The island chain of Indonesia has many often-active volcanos and frequently gets shaken by earthquakes. Sometimes, villages are destroyed, and many lives have been lost.

It takes another day on the train to Jogjakarta. A ticket collector is accompanied by a soldier with his machine gun. I ask if he is going to shoot a hole in the ticket … Due to the extreme poverty, the ticket collector's money is attractive to criminals and, therefore, the need for an armed guard. We sit on the train with our arms on our bags. In Jogjakarta, we visit a bank and have a look around town before we take another train to Surabaya, where we stay at the Hotel Kapasan.

Cock fight

Ticket collector with guard

Cowboy in front of Gunung Agung

A lot of tourist attractions have to be bypassed because of limited finances. The constant travelling along and across the Equator for that many months is highly exhausting. We long for a permanent residence.

On 31 October, we arrive by train in Banjuwangi, situated at the eastern end of Java. It only takes half an hour to cross over by ferry to Gilimanuk in Bali, from where we take a bus to Denpasar at the eastern end of Bali.

Two days are spent exploring Denpasar. With hired Honda motorbikes, we drive around Bali and have a look at the active volcano of Gunung Agung. In 1963, it poured lava down its sides, burying several villages, killing the inhabitants, and turning the whole valley into a black lava desert.

Hired motor scooter

CHAPTER 12:

Travelling to Australia

On 4 November, we find out from a travel agent how to get to Sydney. Once again, we buy air tickets, this time with our last travellers' cheques. Our travel budget was US$3,000 (each) from Johannesburg. We do not want to transfer any more money from our banks at home in Europe. It is better to find work, save some more money, and continue our journey to the Philippines, Japan and Canada. We do not know if we will find work in Australia. But it sometimes pays to be optimistic. Before our departure, there is time to ride around on motorbikes to Ubud in the centre of the island, to Singaradja in the North and to watch a cockfight in Batuan.

Bound for Botany Bay

On 9 November 1970, a six-hour flight in an Australian Qantas plane takes us to Sydney. From the top of the gangway, the blue sky above seems to be much higher than elsewhere. The horizon seems to be wider too. As we walk along George Street in the city, the traffic is heavy, the fumes of cars tickle the nose, and we make our way through crowds of people.

I say to Max, "Oh God! We are back in civilisation."

Our first home in Australia is the Salvation Army Hotel near Central Station.

Our trip from Johannesburg took a little bit more than six months.

We plan to stay for at least half a year to save as much money as possible before we look for more adventures further north, travelling on to the Philippines, Japan, Canada and the USA. We find a flat to rent two days after our arrival and start working within a week.

But after more than fifty years, we still live in Sydney and Brisbane, in the land of "Down Under", and **WE CALL AUSTRALIA HOME.**

www.ingramcontent.com/pod-product-compliance
Lightning Source LLC
Chambersburg PA
CBHW071607080526
44588CB00010B/1055